D0995660

Norwich

History and Guide

Malcolm Atkin

ALAN SUTTON

First published in the United Kingdom in 1993 by
Alan Sutton Publishing Ltd
Phoenix Mill · Far Thrupp · Stroud · Gloucestershire

First published in the United States of America in 1993 by
Alan Sutton Publishing Inc · 83 Washington Street · Dover · NH 03820

British Library Cataloguing in Publication Data applied for

Jacket Illustration: Pull's Ferry, the fifteenth-century water gate into
the cathedral close of Norwich. *(Viewfinder Colour Photo Library)*

Typeset in 10/13 Times.
Typesetting and origination by
Alan Sutton Publishing Limited.
Printed in Great Britain by
The Bath Press, Avon.

Contents

Preface

Norwich has been renowned as a 'Fine City' since George Borrow coined the phrase in 1851. Much of its proud heritage can still be seen in the surviving late medieval and later buildings, dominated by the many medieval churches, in its medieval street names and less obviously, but no less importantly, in its street plan – elements of which date back to its Saxon foundation and beyond that into the Roman period.

This book concentrates on telling the story of Norwich through those physical remains in the hope that the reader and visitor will be better able to appreciate that history. Use is also made of the wealth of surviving documentary evidence for the history of the city. But it has to be acknowledged that the surviving physical remains are a biased source – owing their existence to the vagaries of methods of building construction and wealth. Norwich became a pioneer in the development of medieval and post-medieval archaeology in the 1970s, and the book is also able to draw on the 'new' source of archaeology to explore the history of the settlement into the period before documents were common and into strata of society that have left no conventional history.

But the story of Norwich is perhaps best served when all of the sources – archaeology, documents, standing buildings – can be used together.

CHAPTER ONE

The Geographical Background

The early development of Norwich was shaped by its geographical setting. The site was a natural focus for the agricultural activities of the surrounding region and it also possessed excellent communications further afield by both land and water. It was these factors, seized upon by political opportunism, which allowed Norwich to develop from a collection of farmsteads into the second largest city of medieval England.

The site of the present city lies within a double bend of the River Wensum, at its lowest fording point and just above its confluence with the River Yare. Norwich was, therefore, the furthest point to which cargo could be carried by sea-going vessels, and its importance was accentuated by its position as a natural junction of land routes. The settlement was established on wide and well-drained gravel terraces deposited by the meandering river, between areas of less accessible river marsh, and at a point where the broad river valley was constricted by steep hills to the north-east and south-west – so funnelling traffic.

Norwich is still overlooked by Mousehold Heath to the east and is dominated by the 20 m high steep cliff rising above the line of what is

View of the city from Mousehold Heath in 1819. This clearly shows the commanding heights of the heath. Note the ruins of St Leonard's Priory to the left, and Bishop Bridge is still shown standing. (*Vignette from map by Edward Langley and William Belch*)

1

Although local topography is dominated by the River Wensum, a number of smaller watercourses may also have played a significant role in shaping the pattern of development. The line of the Great Cockey can still be traced as it runs down Little London Street, and can be noted as a dip in the line of Bedford Street. The cockey provided a boundary line and was a source of water and a convenient sewer

now King Street on to Ber Street. Despite the popular misconception of Norfolk being flat, Norwich is in fact one of England's hilliest cities!

The land was divided by a number of streams or 'cockeys' which played a key role in providing natural boundary lines for the settlement and also supplies of water for personal consumption, drainage and industry. The largest of the 'lost' stream courses north of the river was the River Dalimund, which entered the city from Catton between St Augustine's and Magdalen gates, cut across the line of Magdalen Street from Stump Cross and entered the Wensum near St Edmund's church. It may have been large enough to provide a sheltered berth for smaller shipping on the river. To the west, the Muspool rose from a source at the south end of Muspole Street, ran along part of Colegate and entered the Wensum west of Fye Bridge. To the east, 'Spiteldike' rose from near St Paul's church and ran west of Cowgate Street but may then have been diverted to join the Dalimund. South of the River Wensum was the 'Great Cockey', rising from what became known as 'Jack's Pit' on All Saints Green, running down Little London Street (formerly Little Cockey Lane) and entering the Wensum just west of Blackfriars Bridge (following the present dip in the ground which is particularly visible on Bedford Street). Another cockey ran south to north from Bethel Street along Willow Lane, St Swithin's Lane and into the river east of St Margaret's Staithe. Other cockeys ran west to east off what became the lines of King Street and Rose Lane, with the latter on the line of the watershed.

Norfolk has traditionally looked eastwards towards the North Sea, divided as it is from the midlands by the fens. Until the Roman period the main focus of population in Norfolk had been in the west of the county, where the soils were light and easily worked. The development of heavier ploughs allowed the richer but heavier soils of east Norfolk (including those to the south of Norwich) to be opened up for agriculture. This placed Norwich at the junction of a number of different farming regions, each becoming more specialized and therefore needing the services of a central market to exchange the goods that they all required. To the east were the rich alluvial meadows used for grazing sheep and cattle; to the north were the 'corn and sheep' areas of the lighter soils and to the west and south the heavier soils which produced a 'wood and pasture' economy. The river was not only an artery of trade from the North Sea but was also a vital supply of fish for the ancient diet. There were other natural resources to exploit too: plentiful supplies of chalk, flint, iron and timber near at hand encouraged industries to develop.

No other site in Norfolk could match these natural advantages. There were no other ports until the eleventh century. Indeed, much of the site of Yarmouth, built on a sand spit, still lay in the sea until then. Meanwhile, Norwich had been able to carve out a status that was to be unassailable.

But to talk of a town and port is to jump ahead in the story. The history of Norwich began thousands of years before those functions developed.

CHAPTER TWO

The Earliest Settlers

Prehistoric Occupation

There are only shadowy traces of the earliest inhabitants in the area that became Norwich. Hunters are represented by the tools that they lost or hoarded as they moved through the landscape, initially roving beside the river but then settling, at first only seasonally, around temporary clearings where they grew crops.

The earliest evidence of occupation in the area dates back to the Palaeolithic period (400,000 years BC), as represented by scattered finds of simple stone axes from Whitlingham to the south of the city. These would have been used by bands of hunters and fishermen, camping temporarily beside the river and then moving on. With the end of the Ice Age, the weather began to warm up and more open vegetation began to develop, with woodland in the sheltered river valleys. The people were still hunters and gatherers, and flint tools of

The Yare Valley from Whitlingham in the Palaeolithic period, c. 400,000 BC, with a man making a flint hand-axe beside a camp fire. From a display in Norwich Castle Museum

this Mesolithic period have been found in the valley of the River Yare at Trowse and at Arminghall.

It was from the Neolithic period from *c.* 3500 BC that humans first began to systematically change the natural landscape. Using their more substantial flint and stone axes, the Neolithic communities began to clear the woodland to make small fields in which to grow crops such as barley and emmer wheat (the impressions of grains of which are sometimes found in their pots). This more settled way of life has led to a greater survival of information from the period but still no evidence has been found of their timber houses. We do, though, have a better understanding of their thought processes. Ritual was clearly very important to ensure good fortune throughout the farming calendar. A great deal of effort was spent on building the large, circular 'temple' at Arminghall, one mile to the south of what became Norwich. This was similar in type to the stone temple of Stonehenge, but the lack of easily accessible good building stone in the region meant that it was constructed of timber posts and therefore has not survived in a standing form. A large circular bank, 15 m wide and with ditches to each side enclosed an area with a diameter of *c.* 27 m. Within this space was a horseshoe-shaped setting of eight large posts set deep into the ground within large pits. It is likely that this henge served as the focus for population in the vicinity and was an important social centre. Other deep pits found at Eaton have also been described as 'ritual', which archaeologists usually ascribe to things they cannot fully explain! Some flint for their tools was mined locally at Whitlingham or at Grimes Graves, 9.6 km (6 miles) north-west of Thetford, but the Neolithic communities were not isolated and the sources of stone used for some of their axes shows that they were trading with Cornwall, the midlands, Wales and the Lake District.

Around 2500 BC the use of metal produced more efficient tools to further open up the countryside. A number of hoards of Bronze Age metalwork have been found around the area of later Norwich – in Costessey, Hellesdon, Unthank Road and Eaton, but none from the city centre sites themselves. These hoards were probably buried as stores to be reused by travelling smiths. A number of burial mounds are also known from the Bronze Age; two out of an original group of four still survive on Eaton golf course and in 1979 one was excavated at Bowthorpe. This mound originally had a diameter of *c.* 11 m, surrounded by two ditches. The primary burial had been carefully buried in a wooden coffin in the centre of the mound, the head of the deceased resting on a hay-filled cushion, but around the edges of the mound were eleven more secondary burials. Fashions in burial practice changed, and around 1800 BC the burnt bones of a cremation, covered by a large urn, were buried in the now silted up inner ditch.

The trend towards clearing the countryside of woodland for arable farming and pasture continued into the Iron Age. Activity from c. 700 BC seems again to have been concentrated along the valley of the River Yare, with pottery of the period being found around Trowse, Markshall and Arminghall. Society was now becoming more sophisticated and coinage was introduced at least to supplement barter. This was the tribal territory of the 'brave and warlike' Iceni as described by the Roman historian Tacitus, and the concentration of coin hoards around the Norwich area suggests that the capital of one of the subtribes was probably here (spurring the Roman development at Caistor St Edmunds).

Roman Farms

The Romans therefore found a populated and developed countryside, the potential of which they sought to develop. But their plans were disrupted by the revolt of Boudicca in AD 60. As part of the subsequent pacification process the Romans sought to exert their own stamp on the settlement pattern. The town of Caistor St Edmunds (*Venta Icenorum*), lying 5 km to the south of what became Norwich and 3 km from Arminghall, had no obvious Iron Age antecedents and may have served a quite artificial function as the new cantonal capital. This was a function that was not to survive the collapse of the Roman administrative system – creating a vacuum which was a factor of great significance for the emergence of Norwich, which was still simply farmland. After the disruption of the revolt, Iron Age farmers gradually assimilated Roman customs. Traces of Romano-British field systems have been found locally at Eaton, with ditches dividing the land into rectangular fields c. 40 m (130 ft) across and separated by tracks. The Romans brought new improved communications to the countryside and it is from this period that we have the first surviving evidence of the exploitation of the site of Norwich as a route centre (although this may have made use of less clearly defined but nonetheless already existing road lines). A west to east road ran beside the loop in the river to cross at Bishopgate (running from Dereham Road – St Benedict's Street – Bishopgate) and leading ultimately to a port at Brundall. A scatter of Roman coins has been found along its route. There was

Late Bronze Age axes dating to c. 800 BC from a hoard found at Eaton. The hoard was probably hidden by travelling smiths

Roman pot found on the site of a Roman cemetery at the West Norwich hospital, beside the Roman road running towards Brundall. The colour-coated vessel dates to the fourth century

Great Square-Headed brooch dating to the sixth century, from the Eade Road Anglo-Saxon cemetery

possibly also a north to south road from Caistor, crossing a ford at Fye Bridge – but no evidence of this has yet been found along the present routes of King Street or Ber Street.

The only evidence of actual occupation on the site of Norwich during this period, in the form of a thin scatter of Roman pottery, is confined to a possible farmstead on the well-drained gravel soils in the St Augustine's area. A cemetery related to another settlement, however, was found immediately to the east of the city on Harvey Lane in Thorpe, where possible evidence of a Roman ford or wharf was also found on the north bank of the River Yare. The importance of this settlement is suggested both by the presence in the same area of earlier Iron Age material and also by later Anglo-Saxon finds and documentary evidence. There were probably other settlements around the area at Eaton, Earlham and Lakenham.

Early Anglo-Saxon

The collapse of Roman rule in the fifth century was a major cultural trauma for Britain, but it is less certain how far the everyday lives of the inhabitants were affected. Anglian place-names now dominate the region. In some instances the piratical raids of the Angles and Saxons along the rivers of the east coast may have driven out the inhabitants of the Romano-British villages, but in other cases the local peasants may simply have found new Anglian landlords. Archaeological labels of 'Iron Age', 'Roman' and 'Anglo-Saxon' obscure the continuity of everyday life. What is certain is that the great natural advantages of the site were recognized by all comers. To those were now added the legacy of the Roman conquest and the new ease of land communications, offered by the Roman road running east to west beside the Wensum and the possible north to south route.

There is a concentration of Anglo-Saxon cemeteries in the area around Norwich, reflecting the movement of the new settlers up the rivers Wensum and Yare from the North Sea into those areas (around the now abandoned Caistor St Edmunds) that were already centres of population in the Roman period. The only cemetery known from Norwich itself was found in the nineteenth century on Eade Road to the north of the city, but unfortunately little of the material from it has survived. This is a pity because the non-Christian graves contained items that might be needed in the afterlife, which can tell us a great deal about the life of their community. These people, who had come over to Britain first as mercenaries for the Romans and then as pirates, may not have built fine stone houses, left impressive mosaics or have been capable of making fine pottery, but the quality of the metalwork found in the other cemeteries of Norfolk (such as Spong Hill and Morningthorpe) illustrates the high standard of craftsmanship attained in their society.

The settlement to which the Eade Road cemetery was related may have been sited some distance away and there are few clues indicating where this may have been. It may be that a village or collection of farmsteads was not actually settled on one permanent site but that it moved around the district, ultimately settling in one of what became the five Middle Anglo-Saxon settlements of Westwick, Coslany, Northwic, Needham and Conesford. Other Anglo-Saxon material dating from the sixth century has been found near St Benedict's Gate and in the area of St Michael at Plea, suggesting that the earliest settlements may have grown up each side of the river at Coslany (south of the Eade Road cemetery) and Westwick, and further along the Roman road in Conesford. It is also possible that the vestiges of a Roman estate survived in Thorpe as the basis of a Saxon palace (*villa regia*). Evidence of Roman occupation there was succeeded by finds of Anglo-Saxon material and the Domesday manor had outliers spread unusually widely in Arminghall, Catton, Sprowston and Lakenham. Although by then it was in the hands of Archbishop Stigand, if it had originally been a royal holding it might explain the place-name of the 'King's Ford' leading towards it – ultimately giving its name to Conesford.

CHAPTER THREE

Saxon Villages

A s the land became more and more opened up through advances in agricultural technique (particularly with the development of a heavier plough), the wealth of the district could be ever more exploited and more people were attracted into the market area adjacent to the *villa regia* at Thorpe. Groups of farmsteads, perhaps reflecting family groupings, may have begun to join together as part of a trend towards the nucleation of settlement that seems to have occurred later in the ninth and tenth centuries. Probably each component part was initially sited so the land around could be developed without too much conflict. But together they also provided the focus for a market to serve a wider area. The people who traded and made goods for the farmers did not produce food for themselves and there was therefore a mutual reliance of supplier and supplied. Herein is the genesis of a market town.

Thus in the Middle Saxon period of *c.* 650-850 a number of small settlements at Norwich grew up on either side of the river. The period is defined archaeologically by the appearance of a distinctive type of wheel-made pottery called Ipswich-type ware, but we are also able to use place-name evidence. The form of the names Northwic, Westwick and Coslany suggest an origin before 850. *Wic* is an OE suffix denoting a trading settlement or market, providing an idea of the growing importance of the trading function of the area. The earliest known form of Conesford is later, originating after *c.* 900, but it probably represents a Danish modification (*Konungrford*) of an earlier name, referring to the 'King's Ford' – a reflection of the importance of the route that the settlement lay beside. The fifth area is Needham, at the east end of St Stephen's Street. The derivation of the name is from the OE 'poor homestead'. The character and extent of such settlements is still shadowy and has proved to be one of the most enduring of recent archaeological detective mysteries. The distribution of isolated and largely residual, or unstratified, pottery sherds of the period can give a false impression of the scale of the settlement itself. Rather than indicate where the houses were, the pottery might simply indicate the wider spread of manured fields. Indeed, much of

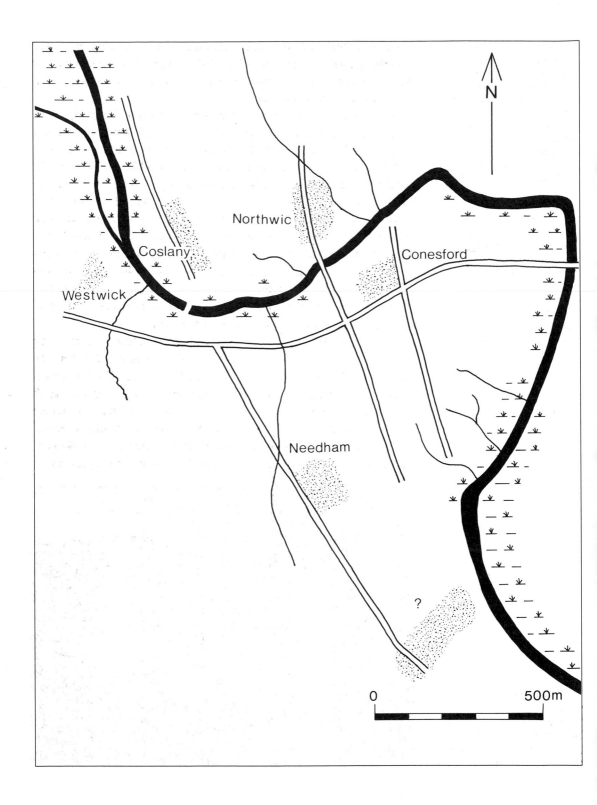

Westwick

Coslany

Northwic

Conesford

Needham

?

N

0   500m

Opposite: Middle Saxon (eighth- to ninth-century) Norwich. Occupation at this time consisted of a number of small hamlets taking advantage of the river and the former Roman route system. The names of some of these settlements, Westwic, Needham, Coslany, still survive as districts of the city, while Northwic gave itself to the name of the later town as a whole. The lines of the former watercourses, or cockeys, running through the area are also shown (omitted on later plans for clarity). The possibility of an unnamed settlement between the south ends of Ber Street and King Street is also shown, although there is, as yet, no definite evidence for this

the information gathered from excavations and watching briefs has been 'negative', in that it has identified where there is *no* evidence of Middle Saxon occupation, therefore narrowing down where that occupation might actually have been!

South of the River Wensum, the largest concentration of Ipswich-type ware is in North Conesford where there may have been a linear settlement of *c.* 2 ha (5 acres) beside an east to west road above the 6 m (20 ft) contour and next to a gravel spur on which boats could be beached. This spur – the medieval *Bychel* – can still be noted as a rise of all of 0.5 m (1½ ft) on St Martin-at-Palace Plain. Until 1987 only fifteen sherds of Ipswich-type ware had been recovered from the suspected area of Needham, although their widely scattered distribution had tended to result in an over-impressive plan of this 'poor' settlement. Considerable sampling of sites in and around the Westwick area has suggested that the likely extent of this settlement was confined to a possible area of only 1½ ha (3½ acres) at the west end of St Benedict's Street (on the line of the Roman road).

There may also have been a small hamlet for which no early name has been passed down to us in the area that became defined by the churches of St John de Sepulchre and St Etheldreda. The former has possible evidence of Saxon building work in its transepts; St Etheldreda was a seventh-century queen of Northumbria and founder of a convent at Ely – making this possibly one of the city's earliest dedications. The church also had remarkably extensive tithes. Work to the east of St Etheldreda in 1975 was unable to suggest the presence of

South spandrel of the west door to St Laurence's church on St Benedict's Street. This depicts the martyrdom of St Edmund, King of East Anglia, who was killed by the Danes in 869

settlement earlier than the twelfth century but experience on the fringes of the Middle Saxon settlements of Coslany and in Westwick has shown how deceptive such small-scale work can be, with the early occupation sites being very tightly contained. It is possible that there was an undocumented settlement with its main core stretching down from St John de Sepulchre to St Etheldreda, so defining a settlement with a similar plan to that suggested for Middle Saxon Coslany. This hypothesis remains to be tested.

The inability to sample areas to the north of the river on a similar scale has been particularly frustrating. There is still no clear evidence for the original extent of Middle Saxon Coslany (OE 'island in a bog'), presumed to extend from the marsh beside the River Wensum north to St Martin's Lane. Ipswich-type ware found in a field soil deposit immediately outside the suggested line of the eleventh-century defences on St Martin's Lane has been interpreted as being imported with manure from occupation further to the south.

. It is to the north of the river, however, that we must look for the genesis of the urbanization of Norwich. It is only here (within a circuit centred on Magdalen Street, see below, p.15), that there is evidence for defences in the tenth century. Logically this might suggest an earlier, Middle Saxon, importance to the area. Despite the obvious attraction of the derivation of the place-name Northwic as being north of the river and its possible ninth-century origin, it has been held that the name developed as a generic reference to encompass the other named Middle Saxon settlements, and was possibly centred south of the river on that already called Conesford. Yet excavation in the latter showed that large-scale development did not begin here until the eleventh century and there is no evidence for it being the prime focus of the settlement. By contrast, excavations on the north bank of the Wensum on Fishergate in 1985 (just to the east of Magdalen Street) provided evidence for a substantial eighth-century antecedent to the tenth-century defended settlement. One hundred and fifty-five sherds of Middle Saxon pottery and a Mercian penny of c. 725 were found. Although these finds were in secondary deposits dating to the Late Saxon period, they suggest the dumping of rubbish from a notable centre of occupation close by. Logic would seem to suggest that this otherwise unnamed early core of settlement is indeed the origin of Northwic, which then developed in the tenth century as the primary focus of urbanization.

Thus, over 400,000 years after people started to live in the area, Norwich itself was about to be born.

CHAPTER FOUR

Late Saxon Town

The name Northwic first appears for certain as a mint mark on coins of Athelstan from 924 to 939. This marks an important stage in the development of the settlement, as a mint could only be sited in a burh – defined as a fortified place with a market. A further indication of the enhanced status of the settlement comes from the later tenth century when Abbot Brihtnoth of Ely (970–96/9) went to Cambridge to buy some land and was told that 'Cambridge and Norwich and Ipswich and Thetford were of such liberty and dignity that if anyone bought land there he did not need witnesses.'

The Middle Saxon villages had probably begun to coalesce as their market functions expanded, but the impetus for the creation of a much larger town was probably political and reflects a new administrative, possibly royal, role for the settlement. The crux of the argument about when exactly this change took place rests on the date of the excavated defences in relation to the Danish invasion of the ninth century. It seems unlikely that they were built by the Danes against the English during the forty years of Danish rule from 879–917. Evidence for Danish involvement in the settlement is slight. There are a number of -gata suffixes to place-names both within the town and also to the south-east, but such names were being formed into the late eleventh and twelfth centuries. The Danes may well have come here to take advantage of an existing market centre but it is not at all clear whether they imbued the settlement with any additional significance. Their influence does not seem to have been strong enough to change the -wic suffixes to -vic as they did at York from Eoforwic to Jorvic. It is more likely that the town was defended after 920, when the English under Edward the Elder regained control of East Anglia and needed a base against any renewed Danish aggression. There may also have been some remodelling of the defences in the late tenth and early eleventh century, first as a response to the sack of Ipswich in 991 and then following the Danish raids of 993, 1004, 1014 or 1016. The *Anglo-Saxon Chronicle* for 1004 describes how 'In this year Swein came with his fleet to Norwich, and completely sacked the borough and

Silver penny of Athelstan (924–39). This is the earliest certain record of the name Norwich (Norwic)

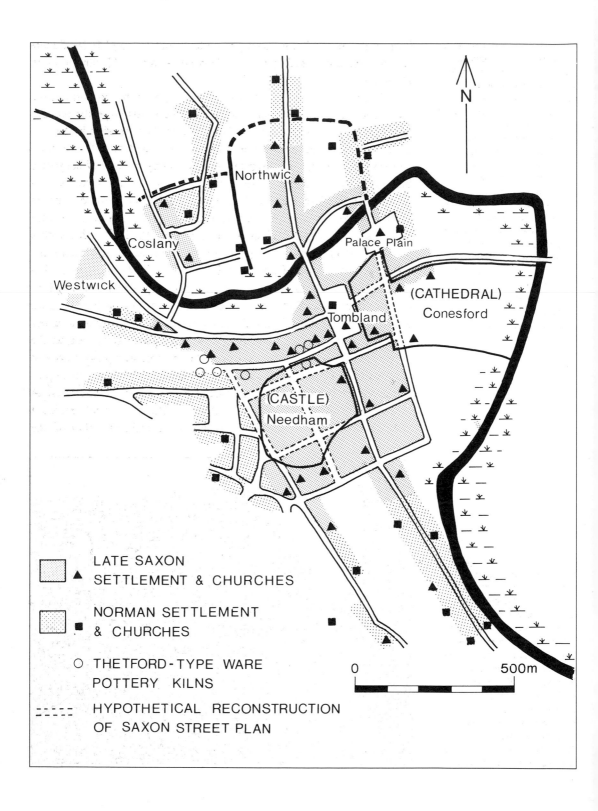

N

Northwic

Coslany

Westwick

Palace Plain

Tombland

(CATHEDRAL)
Conesford

(CASTLE)
Needham

LATE SAXON
SETTLEMENT & CHURCHES

NORMAN SETTLEMENT
& CHURCHES

○ THETFORD-TYPE WARE
POTTERY KILNS

----- HYPOTHETICAL RECONSTRUCTION
OF SAXON STREET PLAN

0   500m

Opposite: Late Saxon (tenth- to eleventh-century) Norwich. North of the river is the tenth-century defended town, possibly linked to Coslany in the eleventh century by a line of defence just north of St Martin's Lane. South of the river is the suggested layout of the eleventh-century planned town. Small suburbs were developing on the main approach roads by 1066 but the plan of the settlement was radically altered at the Norman Conquest. The castle and cathedral were emplanted over part of the Saxon town, while the new Norman borough shifted the commercial focus to the west. But the town thrived and new suburbs quickly developed

burnt it down,' while, following the attacks of 1014 and 1016, Canute was described as the king who 'made corslets [run] red [with blood] in Norwich'.

Evidence of pre-Norman defences has only been found north of the river where elements of their line can still be followed in the modern street plan. The best defined are fossilized on the west side in the parallel lines of St George's Street/Calvert Street and then to the north and east in the curve of Cowgate and possibly by the line of the parish boundary between St Paul's and All Saints. Using such clues, excavation in 1975, 1976 and 1989 revealed a substantial ditch running beneath or east of Botolph Street and St George's Street. The oft-recut ditch was shown to be 'v'-shaped and 6–8 m (18–24 ft) wide with a surviving depth of over 3 m (6 ft). On the east side of the circuit, the outer edge of a similar feature was found during 1978 in a trench adjacent to Jarrold's Printing Works, running directly beneath Whitefriars. On the inner side of the ditch would have been an earthen rampart, perhaps 5 m (15 ft) wide and 3 m (9 ft) high, surmounted by a timber palisade. No evidence of the latter has yet been found because after the defences fell out of use, the soil from the rampart was pushed back to fill the ditch. The resultant hollow in the ground was then taken up as a convenient line for a street (as St George's Street and Whitefriars). A sample from the first recut of the ditch on Botolph Street yielded a radiocarbon date of AD 890±60, but the rectilinear plan of the

View looking north along the line of the tenth-century Saxon defence ditch of Northwic, now marked by St George's Street. On the corner with Colegate is Bacon's House. This courtyard plan merchant's house was built by 1547 and was the home of Henry Bacon, mayor of Norwich in 1557 and 1566. On the Colegate frontage was a shop, buttery and parlour with chambers above, and with an open hall running along St George's Street. One of its later uses was as a tobacco factory

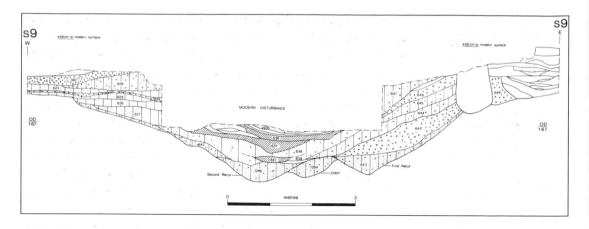

defences is more suggestive of an English, rather than Danish, design. Otherwise finds came from the period of the final demolition of the defences.

Information about what the town was like within these defences is extremely limited. Excavation just within the line of the defences on Cowgate in 1974 revealed only an isolated pit that may have dated to this period, backfilled in the eleventh or twelfth century. The land then remained vacant until the fourteenth century. The absence of any sign of intensive Saxon occupation behind the north and west defences suggests that the settlement was thinly settled around its landward margins, with the land possibly used for protected grazing. But on the south side of the defended enclosure the 1985 excavations on Fishergate suggested a more intense colonization of the river foreshore by, or in, the tenth century. Here the marshy surface was consolidated by wickerwork fencing and an attempt was made to drain it with ditches.

Occupation in Coslany during the tenth century was probably confined to a narrow linear development along the line of Oak Street and towards the river. There are, however, signs that the settlement was expanding in the eleventh century. The location of St Mary Coslany church off the existing Oak Street frontage suggests that this marked a late stage in the eastern expansion out of the area during the late eleventh century.

Earlier suggestions of a tenth-century defended enclosure in Conesford around the curve of Elm Hill, Redwell Street and Bank Street have now being discounted and no evidence has yet been found for any extensive occupation here before the eleventh century. But there may then have been a major replanning of the settlement which shifted the whole focus of the Saxon town. The hypothesis is of a planned town which was created on the basis of the early cores of

Section through the tenth-century Saxon defence ditch on St George's Street. The earliest cut was about 6 m (18 ft) wide and 2 m (6 ft) deep. It quickly silted up and was re-cut at least twice, ending up with a width of about 9 m (27 ft) (Norwich Survey)

Copper alloy brooch dating to the tenth century and found within the cemetery of a Late Saxon church excavated on the Anglia TV site in 1979. It is covered in silver gilt and has a decoration of an interlaced cruciform design

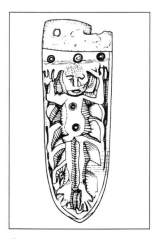

Copper alloy strap-end also dating to the tenth century, and found in a pit on the Anglia TV site. It is decorated with a full-frontal nude figure

Needham and Conesford on land above the 6 m (18 ft) contour, and with alterations to the settlements north of the river to try to bring them within a new unity of development. The model is based on the distribution of Late Saxon pottery and the linear alignment of churches thought to be Anglo-Saxon foundations, together with possible surviving fragments of the Saxon street system which focus on the north-to-south and east-to-west arterial roads and bridging points. The new settlement seems broadly to have been confined to the west by the line of the Great Cockey and to the east by the river marsh, following the limits of Needham and Conesford respectively. The main market was at Tombland (literally 'empty land') lying towards the centre of the town and between the two former cores of settlement.

As yet, there has not been any opportunity to establish the presence or absence of defences around this settlement, but at the moment these seem unlikely. The main wharf of the town at the end of the Saxon period in the eleventh century is presumed still to have been on the north bank of the river within the bounds of the tenth century defences. The replanning south of the river might also have led to a rationalization of the town plan to the north with tenth-century Northwic now being linked to Coslany by a line of new secondary defences found along St Martin's Lane in 1973. This took the form of an undated ditch that was backfilled in the late eleventh or twelfth century.

The conclusion is, therefore, that the focus of both Middle and much of Late Saxon occupation was not, as has long been held, south of the river in the area of the present cathedral Close, but north of the river, focused on the present Magdalen Street – a simple and logical explanation of the place-name Northwic as the 'Northern trading place'. A replanning of the settlement in the eleventh century brought occupation on the south bank to the fore for the first time, in what amounted to the creation of a Saxon 'new town'. It was around the new market on Tombland that the Saxon earl's palace and the wealthiest of the Saxon churches – St Michael's – was now built.

It is likely that, on the basis of pottery distribution and church dedications, small suburbs then began to develop on the approach roads to the town at the very end of the Saxon period – a process that continued into the Norman period until 1075. North of the river, St Augustine's and St Martin at Oak parishes were both cut out of the large parish of St Clement's as settlement developed in these areas. St Olave's church on Pitt Street was sited just outside the line of the putative eleventh-century defences of Coslany with a dedication dating certainly to after 1030 (date of his martyrdom) and probably after 1055 (when it appears in York). South of the river, the churches of St Laurence, St

Margaret, St Swithin and St Benedict, all founded within a quarter mile along St Benedict's Street, may have been cut out of the large parish of St Gregory and represent the (essentially Norman) intensification of settlement along an original ribbon development linking Westwick with the 'new town'. At the start of this process was St Laurence's, the foundation of which can be dated by documentary evidence to before 1038–66, during which time the church owed an annual last of herrings to the Abbey of Bury St Edmunds, and at the end is St Benedict, dated to the late eleventh century on archaeological evidence. The pressure on the street frontage of the suburb stretching out along King Street from the late eleventh century is demonstrated by the siting of St Julian's church off the main street frontage. It is not clear what effect the development of this period had on the putative settlement at the south end of King Street, which may still have been considered as being distinct. The transepts of St John de Sepulchre may date from this, or the early Norman, period.

Evidence of trade and industry in the Saxon town is almost completely restricted to the archaeological evidence and therefore emphasizes those aspects that have left a trace in the ground. Thetford-type ware pottery kilns have been found within the 'new town' along Bedford Street and appear to have originally fronted a secondary street, but the latest of the sequence cluster outside the west entry on East Pottergate – presumably this dirty and fire-prone industry had been forced to move outwards under pressure from the expanding

Saxon Norwich was a major concentration of population and therefore consumption. It consequently became one of the centres of the regional pottery industry making Thetford-type ware. This is a cutaway reconstruction of a pottery kiln of the period

This Thetford-type ware pot was accidentally squashed during manufacture (a 'waster'). The ware was made from the tenth century into the twelfth century and therefore illustrates the continuity of local crafts across the period of the Conquest

Tenth-century carved stone with a decoration of interlaced animals from the site of SS Vaast and Amand on St Faith's Lane. The Flemish dedication of the church suggests that there may have been a colony of merchants from the Low Countries in Late Saxon Norwich

domestic area. Evidence for shoemaking was also found beside the river close-by St Martin-at-Palace Plain. The essence of Late Saxon Norwich was trade. Thus the settlement had moved out of the defended enclosure north of the river and colonized the more exposed river banks on the south bank of the River Wensum, with potential for better land communication. Excavation has shown how ships could berth on the south side of the River Wensum beside St Martin-at-Palace Plain and be dragged up the sandy banks of the river on brushwood matting ready for off-loading on to the raised gravel terrace of Bychel. The church of St Martin-at-Palace Plain was itself known as St Martin *del Hille* or *super montem*. There was a market in Tombland where pottery imported from the midlands, millstones and other pottery from the Rhineland and herrings from the North Sea were all brought for sale. Norwich was already showing its potential as an international port. Other more perishable imports may have included furs and possibly even wild animals from Scandinavia and Russia (the city owed an annual render of a bear to the king) and woollen cloth from Flanders. In return, the inhabitants would have sold local agricultural produce, ironwork and local pottery, wooden and leather objects. There was possibly a colony of Flemish merchants resident here in the eleventh century, with their own church dedicated to SS Vaast and Amand on St Faith's Lane. Although the church was demolished in 1540, a tenth-century cross-shaft was found on the site in the nineteenth century.

A large number of people were still connected with the traditional pursuit of agriculture in an attempt to maintain some degree of self-sufficiency. Norwich contained over 255 ha (630 acres) of farmland at Domesday with the Saxon burgesses holding 32 ha (80 acres) of farmland in the Hundred of Humbleyard. Other areas within the bounds of the later city remained as farming land well into the thirteenth century. By the time of Domesday there were two mills for grinding corn, probably in the Westwick area.

An important element in showing the wealth and importance of Saxon Norwich was the number of churches. By 1066 there were twenty-three to twenty-five, probably including All Saints, St Martin-at-Palace Plain, St Michael Tombland (the wealthiest), Holy Trinity (later to become the cathedral), St Laurence, St Ethelbert, St Gregory, St Clement, St Mary in the Marsh, SS Simon and Jude and possibly St Etheldreda. These were not simply expressions of faith but were important economic investments for their secular founders who took a share of the tithes. One burgess at Domesday held two complete churches and one-sixth of a third. In all, the Saxon burgesses were said to have held fifteen churches. The earliest churches would have been

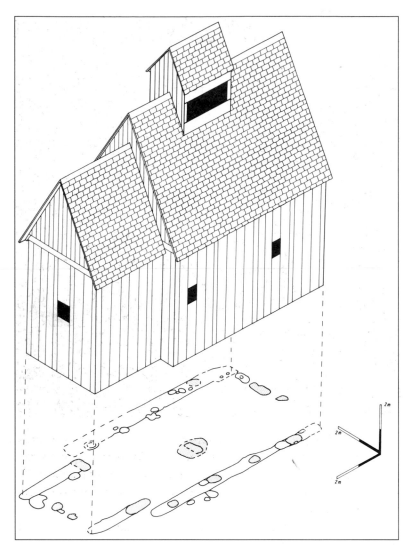

Reconstruction of the eleventh-century phase of the timber church excavated on the Anglia TV site (within the later castle bailey). The structure was built of timber posts set within foundation slots and with the walls possibly made of vertical planks. It may have had a central belfry

made of timber in the tradition of contemporary domestic houses. One was excavated in 1979, along with part of its cemetery, within what became Castle Meadow. When the churches began to be rebuilt in flint rubble from the eleventh century they would have had an even more dramatic impact on the vision of the inhabitants. They were the only stone buildings within the city and their towers would have dominated the skyline. Evidence of Saxon stone churches is complicated by the survival of building styles into the Norman period but includes the distinctive long and short quoins on the chancel of St Martin-at-Palace Plain and at St John Timberhill. Norfolk does not have any source of stone that could be dressed but local masons developed their own

Later Saxon churches were built of flint rubble. The corners of the chancel of St Martin-at-Palace Plain are built from the characteristic Saxon long and short quoins

skills in building with flint. Characteristically the earlier churches have a round tower because it is difficult to build corners in flint without the use of dressed stone quoins. This technique continued into the thirteenth century, however, and none of the Norwich round towers are certainly Saxon.

In summary, five main elements have been suggested for the Saxon development of Norwich.

1) Middle Saxon hamlets at Conesford, Needham and Westwick south of the river and Coslany and Northwic to the north. The possibility of a further hamlet on the south end of King Street has also been noted.

2) Defended tenth-century core centred on present Magdalen Street (the suggested location of Northwic).

3) Eleventh-century (?undefended) town south of river.

4) Partial coalescence of Coslany and Northwic (the former now defended) to complement the new settlement south of the river.

5) Initial development of suburbs south of river (along Pottergate, Ber Street, King Street) and north (around St Augustine's).

By 1065 the special status of Norwich was clear, as it was adminis-
tered separately from the rest of the county, responsible to a royal official who collected the rents and taxes. It had a population of about
5,500, of whom 1,320 were tax-paying burgesses. The latter were
divided among three lordships controlling different parts of the settlement – the King (Edward) and the Earl (Gyrth) (1,238 burgesses),
Archbishop Stigand (50 burgesses) and Harold (32 burgesses). Stigand
was the Saxon Archbishop of Canterbury who retained his position
until 1070. His land was probably on the east side of the town, adjacent to his manor of Thorpe and included part of the land later taken
up as the cathedral precinct. He also held the two churches of St
Michael and St Martin-at-Palace Plain. An indication of the royal
interest in the settlement is possibly suggested by the only park in
Domesday Norfolk, at Costessey. In terms of total area the settlement
spread over most of that later enclosed by the medieval defences
(although with large areas of open space between the cores of occupation). Surrounding the city was possibly the most populous part of
Saxon England and a rich magnet for trade.

St John de Sepulchre church on
the south end of Ber Street. The
transepts of this church contains
possible Saxon windows and
there is also evidence of long
and short work. It may be that
there was a Saxon settlement in
this area (related also to St
Etheldreda's on King Street
below) outside Norwich itself
(*a drawing of c. 1830*)

CHAPTER FIVE

Destruction and Rebirth

The Normans invaded England in 1066. When they descended on Norwich the short term effect was one of considerable destruction. The number of burgesses fell from 1,320 to 719 between 1066 and the Domesday Survey of 1086; thirty-two had fled, with twenty-two of them going to Beccles. There were then also 480 smallholders who were so poor that they paid no dues, and 297 houses were described as destroyed or standing empty.

But a large part of the destruction was caused not by the Conquest itself but by the later rebellion of the Anglo-Norman Earl Ralph de Guader against the king in 1075. Ralph was actually the son of an English father ('Norfolk born' according to Blomefield) and Breton mother, who had quarrelled with Harold and joined the Norman army. His wife Emma was the daughter of William Fitz Osbern. After the rebellion, Ralph and his wife escaped England but the king took out his revenge on the city whose inhabitants were clearly regarded as being implicated in the activities of their partial kinsman. A large area of the city was burned, property was confiscated and the people fined. Some who had been present at Ralph's wedding where the plot was hatched were blinded and others were banished. They also faced an economic penalty in that the annual render to the king was raised from £31 to more than £95. Roger Bigod became constable of the castle but he too rebelled against the succeeding king, William Rufus, and again it was the ordinary people who suffered as he made forays into the surrounding countryside.

Such disruptions, traumatic as they were, only caused temporary interruptions to the development of the town – indicated by the foundation of up to twenty-one churches between 1066 and 1086. This resilience may in itself be a pointer to the status that the Saxon town would have achieved, but in the end it was the Norman Conquest that led to the town realizing its full potential as an international port. Norwich was clearly developing apace in the last years of Saxon rule, but it is impossible to guess how far this development would have occurred without the stimulus that the Normans brought to continental trade. Given the absence of significant quantities of Late Saxon imported pottery from the city, it would appear that the international trading role of Norwich was an essentially Norman phenomenon. Thus it was not called a port in the Saxon period.

King William's intention was clearly that this was no longer to be thought of as a Saxon town. The only recently achieved unity of the Late Saxon town was destroyed, deliberately, by the Norman emplantations of castle, a new borough and cathedral as the Normans sought to put their stamp on the city. The communication pattern of the town was disrupted and the focus of the settlement moved further to the west, leaving south Conesford very much out on a limb. Even so, occupation around St Etheldreda continued and was clearly well established by at least the latter half of the twelfth century, with archaeological evidence of occupation opposite the church (which itself contains twelfth-century work), and to the south was St Edward's church off the street frontage, St Olave's chapel (post-1030) and St Peter Southgate beyond. It therefore warranted being included within the later circuit of defences – giving Norwich its distinctive outline.

Castle

The earliest castle was certainly in existence by 1075. Ninety-eight Saxon houses in the south-west *insula* of the Late Saxon town were destroyed to make way for it. This was a clear symbol of Norman power over the people, serving as the base for the sheriff, the county court, and was a town within a town. The 'Castle Fee' and its inhabitants remained outside city jurisdiction until 1345. The brother of the last Saxon king, Harold, had been Earl of East Anglia and so the building of a Norman castle here was a symbol of the breaking of the Godwin family power – the more so because it was almost certainly local people who would have been expected actually to build it! The castle lies at the north end of the ridge overlooking a new Norman Borough to the west and the English Borough to the north and east, and would have been visible for miles around. Initially the castle was of the motte and bailey type. A timber tower was raised on a partly artificial mound as the ultimate strongpoint, with a flat bailey defended by earthen bank and ditch around it to contain the service buildings. Here would have been the main domestic building (the Great Hall) together with workshops, stables, accommodation for servants and the garrison and even space to graze animals. It was the only royal castle

Eighteenth-century engraving
of the castle. It shows the keep
before the restoration of 1837

in Norfolk and Suffolk until around 1166 – a remarkable situation as
Norfolk and Suffolk were two of the richest shires in the country. The
English reconquest of 917 had been so rapid that there was no need to
establish the network of defended burhs as found elsewhere in the
kingdom. An additional factor was that a large part of Suffolk fell
under the control of the liberties of St Edmund and St Etheldreda, out
of royal control. The Normans could find no other place to equal

Reconstruction of Norwich
castle c. 1200. The surviving
keep is only one part of a
massive complex of defences. It
is ironic that much of the
information about what the
defences of the bailey looked
like comes from the excavations
carried out on the Castle Mall
redevelopment. That
development has in itself
destroyed the ability to
appreciate the keep in its proper
context within its earthen
defences

The defensive ditches of
Norwich Castle were on a
massive scale

Norwich's status and the siting of the royal castle undoubtedly provided a further impetus to development. A stone keep was built around
1100-20, surrounded by more elaborate earthworks, including a horseshoe-shaped barbican with drawbridge leading to a gatehouse, initially
of timber but also rebuilt in stone soon after 1200. The Normans soon
found that they needed their new stone castle. The city was attacked
within this period in 1136 and 1174, and in 1193 the castle contained a
garrison of seventy-five men. Nevertheless, it was seized by Prince
Louis in 1217 and the inhabitants of Norwich must have wondered
how far it protected them – or made them an inviting target! Later, in
1307, John de Lovetot seized £300-worth of cattle from the people of
the district and drove them into the castle.

The Priory and its Precinct

State and Church went hand in hand to stamp the seal of Norman dom-
ination. The priory precinct was created from 1094 after the seat of the
bishopric of East Anglia was moved from Thetford by Herbert de
Losinga. Work started on the new cathedral in 1096. It was designed
to house sixty monks and their servants as the focus of an ecclesiastical empire stretching throughout Norfolk. On the north side of the
cathedral church was the fortified bishop's palace, and on the south
side the monastic service buildings were based around the cloisters. A
canal was dug from the River Wensum into the Lower Close (through

Drawing of the west front of
Norwich cathedral by John
Adey Repton, *c.* 1800

26

the later Pull's Ferry) to carry stone for the building (the church was not completed until *c.*1145). Part of the land was probably already owned by the see – the twelve *mansiones* seized and given by William the Conqueror to the bishop; part (Tombland) was exchanged with Roger Bigod. The east part was later granted by Henry I.

The precinct became a source of great wealth for the city because of the number of penitents visiting the cathedral and the indirect benefit from the business of running the priory estates. But its foundation also excited much resentment (as will be clear from later in its history), for the precinct straddled the east side of the Saxon town which had been devastated in the Norman revolt of 1075 and disrupted its very heart in Tombland, where the earl's palace and St Michael's church were demolished. The cathedral itself was built on the site of the Saxon Holy Trinity church and a crossroad of the eleventh-century town. Excavations on Tombland in 1974 showed how the precinct had otherwise disrupted the east-to-west communication system. It revealed evidence for the original line of Palace Street running towards the river crossing, before its diversion northwards around the priory precinct. There were also traces of buildings, yards and rubbish pits forming part of a service range for the priory just within the precinct wall. Evidence of the early influence of the priory beyond its precinct walls came from the excavations on Bishopgate. Here, the emplantation of the precinct also destroyed the hinterland

Pull's Ferry was the water gate into the cathedral precinct. A canal ran through it to the edge of the Lower Close and was used to bring building materials for the cathedral. The present water gate dates to the fifteenth century, and is next to the sixteenth-century Ferry House

of the possible Saxon market on the south side of St Martin-at-Palace Plain/Bishopgate. The discovery of large quarry pits suggests that a great deal of the land subsequently may have been used for the excavation of sand and gravel as building materials for the cathedral. The Priory, however, also had a more positive effect. It may be that the existing wharf on Bychel was now developed on a grander scale to form part of the private development of the post-Conquest Prior's Fee – explaining the concentration of foreign imports there. In time, this encouraged domestic settlement in the area as part of a 'suburban' development to the precinct.

The Norman church was also responsible for the creation of another new focus of settlement in the town – that of St Paul's Hospital in the north-east of the Saxon town during the bishopric of Eborard in 1121–45. The hospital was accompanied by a parish church and a cluster of seventeen houses.

The French Borough

The French Borough was created in the Mancroft area, just outside the former Saxon town by Earl Ralph de Guader (the new earl of East Anglia) at some point before his rebellion of 1075. Domesday says the land belonged to Earl Ralph who 'granted it to the king in common to make the borough between himself and the king'. It was seized by the king after Ralph's rebellion in 1075. In 1086 there were 125 new French burgesses there, partly making up for the loss of the English burgesses in the rest of the town. But in a marked break from the tradition in the English borough, only three churches were founded here (St Giles, St Stephen and St Peter Mancroft). The lack of competition in the centralized Norman society meant that they all became very wealthy. Most notable of all was St Peter Mancroft. The borough also became the site of the principal market of the city. This was situated on either side of St Peter Mancroft, taking advantage of the main road from London which entered through the later St Stephen's Gate. The creation of the French Borough, although it did not cause the same degree of destruction as the cathedral or castle, was therefore another important element in shifting the focus of the town away from Tombland, to Mancroft and the 'Newport'.

But the Normans brought new trade and prosperity in which the remaining Saxon inhabitants also shared. Despite the political and topographic changes, the archaeological evidence stresses the continuity of ordinary life across the Conquest period. A study of the Thetford-type ware kiln material emphasizes the long life of this

Saxon tradition well into the twelfth century. The use of local masons working on the cathedral is suggested by the way in which round 'Saxon' windows of St Julian and St Gregory are matched in the wall of 1096 or later in the west cloisters of the cathedral. A further example of architectural overlap comes from the use of Caen stone, unlikely to have been imported before the Conquest, in the triangular-headed windows of the round tower to St Mary Coslany. The experience gained on such buildings was then slowly translated into domestic building (albeit initially only those houses belonging to the very wealthiest in the city). The earliest surviving stone domestic building is of the late twelfth century – the Music House on King Street, built for Jurnet the Jew, a wealthy merchant. Another example was excavated beside the river on Palace Plain in 1981.

Trade boundaries increased. The existing trade with the Rhineland continued but now there was the more widespread import of pottery from France and large quantities of building stone from Caen. The

The twelfth-century keep built of Caen stone (restored in 1837) (known as 'Blanch fleur' from the colour of the stone) still dominates modern Norwich. The view is along Davey Place, which was constructed in the early nineteenth century along the line of the King's Head yard

West wall of the infirmary of Norwich Cathedral Priory. It was built *c.* 1096 but its use of double-splayed round windows without the use of dressed stone suggests the work of Saxon masons

influx of a new consumer population encouraged both old and new trades and industries; leather-working, for example, was probably the most extensive industry in the town at this time. An early, though probably exaggerated, sign of what was to become the dominance of the textile industry was provided by a comment from the French chronicler, Jordan Fantosme, who explained the easy capture of Norwich in 1174 by Hugh Bigod and his Flemings by saying that the population 'for the most part were weavers, they knew not how to bear arms in knightly wise'.

The economic growth of the town during this period is shown by further topographic development. The detailed study of evidence from

The triangular-headed double belfry windows in the round tower of St Mary Coslany appear typically Saxon, but the use of Caen stone in their shafts suggest that they were actually built after the Norman Conquest. Round towers were built in Norwich into the thirteenth century

a number of sites has suggested that intensive settlement along St Benedict's Street, once thought to represent Late Saxon ribbon development, was essentially an early Norman creation. It was associated with the well-documented increase in the number of Domesday churches, but had a Saxon precursor in St Laurence and possible scattered settlement around it (on the margins of the eleventh-century town). On the other end of the street, the discovery of burials predating the late eleventh-century church of St Benedict's suggests that this may have formed an outlier of a continuation of the Westwick settlement. It might be argued that at least part of the reason for this rapid expansion along St Benedict's Street was the displacement of the population from the areas of the castle and cathedral. But the number of churches cannot simply be used to suggest (as it has been in the past) that there was a corresponding density in domestic occupation along the street. The number of the churches is a reflection, rather, of the wealth of the various landowners along the street. The land beside St Benedict's church was open space used for extensive quarrying and for farming until the fourteenth century. The use of land for such anti-social activities is a feature of under-developed and secondary settlement areas in Norwich.

The Landgable tax is indicative of the growth of the Norman town. This was a $1d$ rent imposed on property in existence 1066– c. 1090. It had been thought that this might reflect Late Saxon patterns of occupation, but excavation at the south end of King Street and along St Benedict's Street has shown that intensive settlement did not commence in these areas until the late eleventh/early twelfth century – as ribbon suburbs outside the core of the Norman town. Similarly, occupation did not extend outside the Coslany settlement until the mid-twelfth century (as shown by excavations on Oak Street in 1977). A concentration in the north-east corner of the Northwic defences reflects the presence of the extramural hamlet of Pockthorpe.

As the exploitation of the waterfront became more extensive and organized there was a development of riparian streets, dividing the burgeoning riverside industrial activity from domestic occupation behind. Such streets include Elm Hill and Worlds End Lane on the east side of the town and a putative lane on Peel Mews (Westwick Street) to the west. Excavation on Bishopgate and St Martin-at-Palace Plain revealed no evidence of domestic occupation on the river side of this road system. On Westwick Street (Peel Mews) and off Coslany Street the number of horn cores found in eleventh- and twelfth-century contexts suggests that the marsh on both sides of the river might first have been colonized by small-scale horn-workers along the river frontage, with waste ground behind. The distinct mirroring of plan between the excavated tenements of the thirteenth century on Peel Mews suggests that these may then have been laid out as part of a unified scheme of redevelopment by one owner, reflecting an increasing density of settlement in the area from that time onwards; properties fronting both Westwick Street and the River Wensum were possibly separated by a lane. Such a double line of development along the river is documented to the east in the later fourteenth century, but was probably earlier in origin.

The new Norman settlers were soon absorbed; the two communities had merged by at least 1158 with the likelihood that English merchants also traded in the Norman market well before that. The Normans also introduced a wider racial mix in the city, adding an influx of Normans, French, Bretons and Flemings to the Anglo-Danish population of 1066, making this a notably cosmopolitan city. In the time of Richard I a rhyme stated 'For Danes and Irish, Norwich much

The Church institutions not only provided spiritual comfort. They were the medieval world's only equivalent to a health service, running a number of hospitals. This is the twelfth-century Leper Hospital outside the town, on the junction of Sprowston Road and Gilman Road

is fam'd.' By 1144 there was also a community of Jews who had emi-grated from France and the Rhineland under the king's protection. They mainly concentrated in the Haymarket/Saddlegate area, under the shadow of the protection of the royal castle. The wealthiest, Jurnet the Jew, however, mentioned above, lived in a large stone house, Music House, on King Street. They fulfilled an important economic function as moneylenders to the rich and powerful, including the church, and became some of the wealthiest in contemporary society. Although there is no proof, it is quite likely that they helped finance the building of Norwich Cathedral; they certainly lent money to the abbey at Bury St Edmunds. This inevitably caused resentment, and anti-semitic riots were whipped up at intervals in the expectation that, in the process, records of old debts might be destroyed or that bribes would be received in return for future protection. The most infamous case came in 1144 when the Jewish community was accused of the ritual murder of the boy William, a skinner's apprentice, who was subsequently made a saint. A chapel was built on the site of his alleged burial which is now marked by an earthwork beside Mousehold Lane. His tomb was the focus of a number of supposed miracles. The subsequent history of the community was one of mixed fortunes, with the circulation of further horror stories culminating in the synagogue being burnt in 1286. In 1290 Jews were expelled from the country, but by then there were only seven-teen Jewish households left in the city.

Most domestic buildings in Norman Norwich were built of timber. Only the wealthiest in society would have been able to afford the luxury of a stone building at this period. One such person was the wealthy merchant Jurnet the Jew who built the Music House on King Street c. 1175. The building was reconstructed in the fifteenth century. Its name derives from its use as a rehearsal room for the Norwich Waits, the city's official musicians from the sixteenth to the eighteenth century

The remains of another twelfth-century stone building were discovered unexpectedly on the riverfront during excavations on Palace Plain in 1981. The walls (surviving to a height of over 2 m) of a part-cellar, 15 m by 8 m, were built of coursed flint with corners in freestone imported from Northamptonshire. The arch in the foreground of the picture allowed a cesspit above it to be flushed by the adjacent river

The unity of the town by the mid-twelfth century is signalled by fragmentary evidence of the first medieval town defences enclosing both French and English boroughs, initiated by the political troubles of the time. In the reign of King Stephen (1135–54) the burgesses dug 'a new ditch outside the town' which was probably a ditch and rampart along the line of the later defences. They seem to have had little military effect. Hugh Bigod lost the constableship of the castle to Stephen's son, William de Blois and then moved to and fro in allegiance to Stephen and Maud during the civil wars. He regained possession under Henry II but then took part in a further rebellion, sacking the city (which remained loyal to the king) in 1174, refortifying the castle and garrisoning it with Flemish troops.

CHAPTER SIX

The Medieval City

The late twelfth century saw Norwich established as one of the major towns of medieval England. By the late thirteenth century the population may have been anywhere from 5,000 to 10,000, its inhabitants following over 130 trades. There was, however, a price to pay for such accumulation of wealth, as Norwich again became a target for the disaffected. In 1217 the French Prince Louis seized Norwich castle and plundered the city. When Norwich was sacked in 1266 by the 'disinherited' barons the plunder was said to have filled 140 carts and to have been worth 20,000 marks. By 1334 it was the sixth wealthiest town in the country, which continued to see physical expression in the provision, for example, of large fireproof undercrofts in a number of merchant houses (e.g. Bridewell, Strangers Hall) that acted as store rooms and strong rooms. The town continued to earn wealth through its traditional role as a market centre but this was now further advanced by its central administrative role both for secular government and for the Church.

The fourteenth-century undercroft of Strangers Hall, dating to *c*. 1320. It was used to provide a fireproof storage for the L-shaped plan house above

From Town to City

Norwich was now wealthy enough to buy privileges in a series of charters that formally established it as a city. The earliest surviving record of a Royal Charter is from *c.* 1158 by Henry II. But this only confirms the customs and liberties as granted in the time of Henry I without identifying what those actually were, and describes the town as still 'governed in the same way as Beccles and Bungay'.

A major change came on 5 May 1194 when Norwich obtained a charter from Richard I which gave it rights of self-government. This was also regarded later as sanctioning the change of the status of the *burgus* to *civitas* and Norwich might properly be described as a city from that point. It could now commute its various rents and tolls due to the Crown for a fixed annual sum of £108. Its citizens had freedom from tolls throughout England; the city could enjoy the same liberties and privileges as those of London. Most significantly, they could elect their own reeve who would collect the dues and preside over the borough court and assemblies, rather than through a royal official. An entry in a pipe roll of the same year describes them as now 'having the city in their hands'. Another right was that they were no longer obliged to settle cases by duel. William Noche took advantage of this in 1249 when accused of murder – choosing instead to be tried by a jury of thirty-six men (eighteen each from north and south of the Wensum).

A further development in the status of the city came around 1223 with the creation of the four bailiffs who were to maintain order through the four leet courts of Mancroft, Wymer, Conesford and *Ultra Aquam* (north of the river), and who were responsible to an assembly of all the citizens (rather than to a city council) through the *hustengemot* – the origin of the modern hustings. In 1256 came the 'Return of Writs' which gave the citizens the right to try claims for debts through their own court rather than at Westminster. The city's elected representatives rather than royal officials now governed Norwich in the royal name. But the city was not all in their own jurisdiction. A major step forward came when the city gained control of most of the Castle Fee in 1345 (but still excluding the keep, mound and Shire House). The most bitter tensions were with the cathedral priory. The priory accused the city of trespass when constructing the new defences of 1253 and the city disputed the priory's jurisdiction in Tombland, Holmestrete, Newgate and Norman's Hospital. This culminated in one of the great catastrophes in the city's history – the riot of 1272.

The Riot of 1272

The monks claimed that Tombland and its market rights were outside the control of the Domesday town, but the city claimed the area as being under their jurisdiction through the charter of Richard I and by virtue of it being enclosed in the city defences of 1253. A long period of bitter wrangling culminated in the summer of 1272 when the citizens, 'at the instigation of the devil' according to the chronicle of Matthew of Westminster, stormed the Close, burned down the church of St Ethelbert that lay within it, together with many of the wooden service buildings of the Priory, and killed some of the prior's servants.

Ethelbert Gate, built in 1278 at the south end of Tombland as part of the reparations for the citizens' assault on the cathedral precinct in 1272. The chamber above the gateway served as a chapel to replace the church of St Ethelbert that was burnt down in the attack. It is built of flint and freestone with flushwork decoration on the gable. This drawing by A.C. Fayerman shows the gate before its restoration in the nineteenth century

Trouble had come to a head during a tournament on 3 July when there was an affray between young men of the city and men of the priory, each wielding pieces of broken lances as weapons. One of the towns-folk, Adam de Newenton, was killed in the disturbance but his assailants were able to retreat into the cathedral precinct and so out of city jurisdiction. The Norwich coroner held an inquest and two of the prior's men were eventually arrested when they stepped out of the pro-tection of the precinct. For this the prior excommunicated the citizens and bad feeling intensified. Priory servants were also accused of rob-bing a local merchant and drinking, or pouring away, the wine of Hugh le Bromham's tavern. Eventually the citizens besieged the priory to demand justice. But the priory's reply, on 9 August, was to lock its gates, hang shields as symbols of defiance on its walls and fire at passers-by with crossbows. The city retaliated by firing blazing arrows from the tower of St George Tombland. Dominican friars tried to mediate but with no success. Finally the citizens piled up reeds and wood against the precinct gates, burnt them down, and stormed the Close. The priory bakehouse and stables were burnt down along with St Ethelbert's church. The citizens, however, claimed that some of the damage was not their fault. They insisted that priory servants had left a watch fire burning in the Cathedral belfry; this got out of hand and so burnt down not only the belfry but also part of the cloisters including the dormitory, refectory and infirmary. Thirteen of the prior's servants were killed in the riot. The prior himself escaped to Yarmouth and returned with men to try, unsuccessfully, to retake the priory by force. The bishop then sought spiritual sanctions and excommunicated the city. The king could not allow this anarchy to remain unpunished and sent down Hugh Peche, Geoffrey de Percy and another to take charge of the city, he himself arriving later. The king clearly saw there was fault on both sides and the prior was imprisoned until he agreed to resign. But the worst consequences were reserved for the citizens. Twenty-nine people were hanged and drawn for their part in the attack on the priory. Others were dragged around the streets behind horses until they were killed. The woman who was seen to lay the first torch against the priory gate was burnt alive. Others fled. The hard-fought (and paid-for) liberties of Norwich were withdrawn and not restored until 1276. The city was fined 3,000 marks and was forced to build Ethelbert Gate as reparation. The chapel above the gate acted as a sub-stitute for the church destroyed in the riot. The dispute over Tombland rumbled on until in 1306 there was a compromise whereby the area was divided into four parts during fairs, with the citizens and priory each taking a share of the profits.

New Town Defences

One way of showing the growing independence and importance of the town was by the construction of impressive new defences to replace the simple bank and ditch of the mid-twelfth century. These were not just a military defence but served as an economic barrier with which to control traders coming into the city and also were a demonstration of the prestige of the city. They also served as a barrier in time of plague and epidemic. The enclosed area of the medieval town was about one square mile, making it the largest in England.

A new bank and ditch was dug from 1252–3. Excavation has shown the ditch to be over 18 m (60 ft) wide and up to 8.3 m (27 ft) deep, dug in front of a rampart that would have been originally surmounted by a timber palisade. The circuit had nine gates, presumably also built of timber. The defences enclosed a broad sweep from Magpie Road and Baker's Road on the north to the River Wensum and to the south along the line of the present Barn Road, Grapes Hill, Chapelfield Road and

Earlier town defences consisting of a simple bank and ditch were replaced from 1297 to 1344 by a flint wall on top of the earlier bank. Much of the work was paid for by Richard Spynk who gave his name to this tower beside the site of St Stephen's Gate

The fourteenth-century defences included protection across the river, by means of strong chains of Spanish iron strung between boom towers. This is the pair at Carrow, just downstream of the city. The right-hand tower was later used as a coke oven to supply fuel for the nineteenth-century maltings. (*An engraving of a drawing by J. Stark*)

Queen's Road. It therefore enclosed all of the earlier Saxon developments together with large areas of intervening open space such as Gildencroft north of the Wensum, Chapel Field to the west, the Butter Hills to the south and the meadows east of the cathedral. The defences can, therefore, give a misleading impression of the actual size of the settlement, but they are a mark of the confidence of the citizens in enclosing such a huge area. The distinctive elongated shape to include the occupation at the south end of King Street stresses the importance felt for that area as compared with the only newly developed suburb of Heigham (from *c.* 1225) which was excluded.

Such defences were not welcomed by all and the people from the surrounding countryside complained that the defences had interrupted their common ways, whereas before they had entered and left the town without hindrance. By this they meant that they were now expected to pay tolls!

Spurred by threat of French invasion and the sack of the city by the 'disinherited', the defences were improved from the end of the thirteenth century, paid for largely by the local merchant, Richard Spynk. These new defences would have looked very different from all that had gone before. Between 1297 and 1344 a whitewashed flint rubble wall was added on top of the earth bank – a mammoth task requiring about 37,000 tons of flint and the resources of not only masons but also hauliers and miners. Access up the river was prevented by a chain of Spanish iron strung between circular boom towers on each bank. There was also a fence along the river bank. In addition there was the Cow Tower, built within the loop of the Wensum on the Great Hospital's meadow by 1278 and rebuilt in the 1390s. This detached tower may have been an early artillery bastion. It is actually built of flint but has a deceptive brick facing. Spynk also paid for thirty 'espringolds' or catapults, each with a hundred large balls to fire and four great crossbows. The city now had twelve gates which were roofed. In gratitude to Richard Spynk the city agreed that neither he nor his heirs should be forced to take any office and that they should be freed of all taxes and tolls forever.

The Cow Tower protected the great bend of the Wensum and probably carried early artillery. Its present form dates to the 1390s and it is built of flint with a brick facing

The defences were quickly abused, however. In 1344 there were complaints of animals grazing in the ditch and damaging it, and people hanging cloth to dry from the walls.

Use of Space within the Medieval City

The city did not significantly expand outside these defences until the nineteenth century (Norwich only had small suburbs in Heigham and Pockthorpe). Instead it gradually colonized the gaps between the existing settlement cores. This allowed the distinctive outline of medieval Norwich to be firmly fossilized in the modern street plan. A notable factor in the infilling was the settlement of the friars from the second quarter of the thirteenth century. The Dominicans and Franciscans arrived in 1226, the White Friars in *c.* 1256 and the Austin Friars by 1290. Initially they lived very simply within rented houses, using parish churches for their services. But their popularity came to demand large preaching halls and soon they were to expand to be major landowners in the city. The largest precinct was held by the Dominicans (Black Friars). Their original site was north of the Wensum around Colegate but they moved south of the river *c.* 1308 on to what had been the house of the Sack Friars, retaining the old site as gardens (briefly returning there 1413–49 after a disastrous fire). The Austin Friars and Franciscans both took large sites in Conesford (beside St Faith's Lane and Rose Lane) in an area that was increasingly out on a limb and where land was correspondingly cheap. Here they could absorb existing roads, houses and even parish churches. The Carmelites established themselves on Cowgate (the undercroft of one of their buildings now survives as a printing museum). Apart from the major orders there was a host of smaller foundations and also the

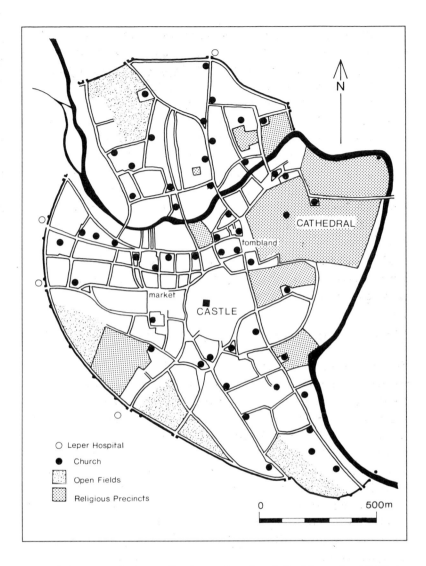

Medieval Norwich, *c*. 1350. It shows the extent of property owned by the church in the medieval city, and also the large area of open fields

establishment of the collegiate church of St Mary in 1248 in Chapelfield, originally founded as a hospital, and to the east the Great Hospital in 1249, originally established to take care of poor, sick or retired chaplains – both founded on what had been open ground.

Other open spaces were taken up with a large number of busy markets, sited around the (still surviving) main provisions market in Mancroft. This was where town and country met. The surrounding villages supplied food and agricultural raw materials for crafts and in return the city provided a wide range of finished goods produced both locally and also imported from all over the known world. Each market had its own speciality. The main provisions market was beside the

The Sorth Prospect of
Black-friers Church in
Norwich.

Ne frustra Quærant Nepotes
Æternitat dicant
THO: PETTVS Baronettus

Guildhall, livestock and cheese were sold south of St Peter Mancroft, horses in Rampant Horse Street, pigs on Orford (Hog) Hill, timber on All Saints Green. The selling of goods elsewhere was strictly controlled to ensure fair dealing, with especial concern being shown for the woollen trade.

The city contained workers in all stages of the leather industry from butchery, skinners, tanners to the producers of finished goods, the most numerous of whom were the shoemakers. Tanners were concentrated north of the river, taking advantage of the three streams running into the river from that side – the Muspool, the Dalymond and Spitaldike. South of the river, the industry gave its name to Barkeres Fleet, which ran through North Conesford.

The textile industry still lagged behind the leather workers in this period in terms of numbers involved and, in contrast to later periods, only a small number of weavers was represented. Norwich may have been principally a finishing centre for cloths at this time employing drapers, followed by dyers, linendrapers, fullers, shearmen, woad merchants and quilterers. Again, most were concentrated beside the river which provided the large supplies of water required for the industry. The dyers were concentrated to the west in St Gregory's sub-leet, especially

The earliest view of the medieval Blackfriars is this south prospect of the late seventeenth century. It was originally prepared for Dugdale's *Monasticon Anglicanum*

44

A thirteenth/fourteenth-century industrial complex was excavated on Alms Lane in 1976. It contained an iron-working complex of smithing and smelting on the St George's Street frontage (right) and a brewing industry on the Alms Lane frontage (top). The activities on the site highlight the problems of identifying *occupiers* as well as the documented *owners*, as the site was owned by a series of leather-workers at the time. Domestic settlement first spread on to the site in the fifteenth century

in the parish of St Laurence where Letestere (Dyers') Row (now Westwick Street) is recorded from 1307. Excavation on Peel Mews (Westwick Street) in 1972, however, has suggested that dyeing was actually undertaken from the twelfth century onwards. Long tenements stretched back from the river and contained a number of large hearths which had traces of madder within them. Long clay-walled structures found here may have been a row of dye-houses, served by a side passage which ran down to the river. Two of the excavated properties were amalgamated by Robert le Weyder in 1299. The property reached the peak of its documented fortune during the late fourteenth and fifteenth centuries when it passed into the hands of the influential Cobbe family. It may well have been this family which was responsible for the construction of the well-built series of furnaces dating from the late fourteenth century that were presumed to have heated the lead dyeing vats referred to in Reginald Cobbe's will of 1384. The latter refers to a 'capital messuage with appurtenances in which I now live with all lead vessels built therein and all other vessels, tools for cloth making, goods and chattels'. The nearby Maddermarket, where that type of dye was sold, also reflects this industry.

A smaller number were engaged in the actual manufacture of clothing. Until the fourteenth century Norwich was probably producing heavy woollen cloths made from short-staple wool fibres. The lighter worsted cloth, made from long-staple wool, is known from 1315 and the two industries continued side by side for some time. The tenter-grounds of the growing textile industry required large open spaces. Medieval cloths were up to 22 m (22 yds) long and there are late thirteenth-century references to *tentorium* 120 ft by 15 ft in St Giles's parish. Tombland was also used to lay out ropes under manufacture (a ropewalk).

The third large group of occupations was connected with supplying the rest of the population with food and drink – the bakers, fishermen, butchers, tavern-keepers, cooks, poulterers, spicers and also the apothecaries. Naturally they appear most commonly around the Mancroft and Tombland markets. Butchers were concentrated in the Ber Street sub-leet, on the route taken by the cattle entering the city to the main markets.

The tradition of metalworking went back to Saxon times. A large number of the smiths were concentrated north of the river, where there had earlier been a widespread smelting industry. For the more wealthy members of society it was possible to buy luxury items from the goldsmiths, harness makers and an armourer based around the Mancroft market.

A great deal of the raw materials would have been supplied locally or imported from the midlands and the North of England, but the city was also able to draw on an extensive continental trade. Imports for industry included steel from Sweden, France and Spain, building stone from France, olive oil from Spain, millstones from the Rhineland, dye-stuffs from the Far East. Luxury goods included wine from Gascony and silks from Italy and the east, but some more basic commodities were also imported, such as salted herrings from Scandinavia and pottery from the Low Countries and France.

The city had space to spare but there is evidence from the fourteenth century of greater pressures being put on land-use. Domestic settlement now spread on to land at the west end of St Benedict's Street that was referred to as *duabus acris terrae aribilis* ('two acres of arable land') in 1160 and had also been used as open quarries. Land speculation was also revealed on excavations on Oak Street, where the first intensive development of the street frontage also took place in the late thirteenth/early fourteenth century, and documentary evidence informs

The only surviving medieval bridge in Norwich is the three-arched Bishop Bridge, dating from *c.* 1340

us that one of the properties was sold five times between 1300 and 1313. Such expansion was an opportunity for the city to accrue new revenue and in 1329 there was a dispute with the Crown as to who was entitled to the rents from buildings constructed on what had previously been waste ground. Nevertheless, large areas of the city within the city walls were undeveloped until at least the fourteenth/fifteenth century and Norwich remained known as a 'city within a garden'.

As great a resource as the river was to industrial and domestic activities, it could also be a barrier to a growing town and Norwich built more bridges than any other medieval town in England. Those bridges that are probably pre-Conquest in origin (Fye Bridge and Whitefriars Bridge) define the upper limit of navigation, and the construction of Bishop Bridge downstream before 1269 therefore enables us to chart the movement of the wharves on to King Street. Bishop Bridge is now the only surviving medieval bridge in the city.

Medieval Houses and their Occupants

We rely almost entirely on archaeological evidence for information of how the inhabitants of Norwich actually lived at this time. But many of the poorest quality houses have left no trace. Some were so insubstantial that in 1290 a flood 'overturned some houses and bore them along'. Most buildings of the late eleventh to thirteenth century were of timber, set in post-holes or with slots for sill-beams. By the thirteenth/fourteenth century such buildings were being rebuilt with a mixture of clay and timber-walling. These were not simply the poor quality houses of the artisan classes: examples included the property built c. 1332 as the town house of the Abbey of North Creake on Oak Street, which was built with flint rubble walls on the main frontage but with clay walls on the more hidden sides of the building. Some of the timber-framing was carried on flint rubble plinths; a rising minority of higher quality buildings had ground floors entirely built of flint. In 1285 Nicholas de Ingham and his wife granted to their son, Walter, 'all their stone houses' in Fyebridge Street (*omnes domos suas lapideas*).

There was little social zoning as rich and poor lived side by side – but in very different conditions. Surviving later medieval buildings tend to be those of the upper strata of society and were built on a multi-roomed courtyard or right-angled plan. The medieval norm, however, as shown by excavation in Norwich, was of simply one or two 4 m-square rooms. Shared occupancy of rooms was probably common among the poor. (In a post-medieval example, one house in St Paul's parish housed eight families.) The houses were originally

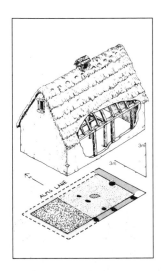

The small number of surviving medieval houses in the city – representing the homes of the urban elite – are timber-framed, with flint ground-floor walls (see Pykerell's House or Pettus House). In contrast, many of the city's medieval buildings were built with clay walls, or used clay to infill between timber uprights. The clay itself was laid in thin layers between shuttering. The technique seems to have been abandoned after the fires of 1507. This reconstruction is based on one of the best, a fifteenth-century example, with a plan of two rooms, which was excavated on Alms Lane in 1976

Pykerell's House on St Mary Plain. This is the classic impression of a late medieval house, built on a right-angled plan with a jettied upper storey and still with its thatched roof. In fact this type of house was the exception rather than the rule. It was built *c.*1500 for a wealthy mayor of the city, Thomas Pykerell. We must look to excavated examples for an idea of how the majority of people lived

single storeyed although a loft or a first floor was often added in the later medieval period.

There was little restriction on street frontage space away from the centre of the city and so most buildings were ranged parallel with the street frontage. Many of the early buildings were unheated although a variety of open hearths or rudimentary fireplaces were soon added. There is a contemporary description of a house in Fyebridge Street in 1263. It was built around a courtyard, and the range next to the street was either a workshop or store room. The main room was the hall where meals were eaten and also where the males of the household slept. Off this was the chamber where the more valuable possessions were kept; it was also the sleeping quarters for the women. There is no mention of heating, so cooking was probably carried out in the courtyard.

If most of the medieval houses have disappeared, their legacy still remains in the pattern of medieval tenement boundaries. In many cases the 1885 OS Map and many modern property divisions can be shown to accurately reflect the division of tenements stretching back as far as the twelfth/thirteenth century, although this can be complicated by the subdivision of older tenements and by the presence of large shared yards. On an excavation it is frequently the character of the yards, and the finds from within them, that can offer the best clues as to the actual status and use of the property. The industrial range and yard areas of

Excavation in 1987 of the medieval cemetery of St Margaret *in combusto* on Magdalen Street. Some 436 articulated skeletons and the remains of up to 600 others were found. Many of the skeletons were probably the remains of executed criminals. Note the individuals buried face down, one with hands behind his back as if tied together

the dyeworks survived on the Westwick Street excavation from the twelfth century through to the seventeenth century, with a series of rebuilt and repaired hearths, furnace bases, drains and wells. Most of the tenements drew their water supply from wells in the rear yards, although the river itself, dirty as it was, remained an important source of supply well into the post-medieval period. Digging wells could be dangerous. In 1279 Thomas Dust, a wellmaker, was being lowered into a well in the courtyard of Henry de Senges, but he fell out of the bucket and died of the foul air at the bottom of the shaft. There is a change in the general nature of the domestic yard areas during the medieval period. The characteristically heavily pitted earlier yards were used as regularly shifting rubbish areas, but this was discontinued in the later medieval period on the widespread introduction of more permanent sanitary arrangements, comprising cesspits either built within the houses or attached to the rear walls. But most rubbish found its way out into the street, into the cockeys or into the river

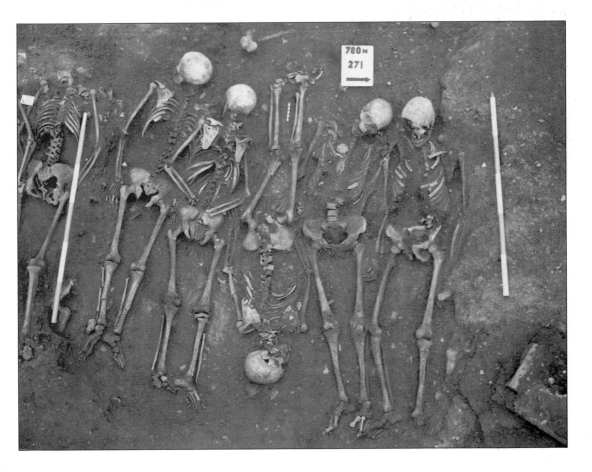

itself. In the leet roll for 1288 the anchorite of All Saints had stopped up the cockey with rubbish 'so that no one can pass by there'.

Medieval Norwich was therefore a dirty, smelly, and often a violent, place. In 1263 Katherine, widow of Stephen Justice, accused eight persons of breaking into her house, robbing it and burning the dead body of her husband which was lying on its bier before his funeral. In the following year Mark de Brunhalle and Ralph Knicht threatened to cut the coroners 'into little pieces' unless they destroyed the record of an inquest on two murdered persons. Rather bizarrely, Ralph de Hadestock (an approver in Norwich castle) accused two men and two women of receiving stolen goods from him – but not paying for them. (An approver was a guilty man who was pardoned in return for securing the conviction of other felons.) Excavation of the cemetery of St Margaret *in combusto* on Magdalen Street, the church known as *ubi sepeliuntur suspensi*, 'where those who have been hanged are buried', revealed the burials, dating between 1100 and 1468, of a number of individuals thought to have been hanged.

Yet at the time Norwich was an attractive place for many to emigrate to. Many of the population *c.* 1300 seem likely to have been recent immigrants from the surrounding countryside. The surnames of those mentioned in deeds of the period contain frequent references to local villages, most within a twenty mile radius. Over 70 per cent of villages within a ten mile radius of Norwich were providing immigrants according to the evidence of the 1285–1311 deeds; more than 400 villages in Norfolk and a further 60 in Suffolk are mentioned. They came with or without permission. If a serf managed to remain in the city for a year and a day then he could not be returned to his lord.

CHAPTER SEVEN

After the Black Death – Late Medieval Norwich

Disease and Sanitation

This period in Norwich's history began with the natural disaster of the Black Death and ended with the close of the man-made disasters of the Wars of the Roses. Various epidemics, lumped together as 'plague', were endemic in medieval England. But the Black Death that appeared in January 1349 was recognized as being something special both in terms of the speed with which it acted and the numbers that it killed. It therefore formed a watershed in the lives of those living in Norwich. The disease was actually bubonic plague accompanied by pneumonic plague, and was spread by the fleas of the black rat which were forced to leave their natural hosts for humans after the rats died. For this reason the rat catcher was an important element of medieval society. In 1388–9 40*d* was paid to John Ratoner for his efforts. The total death toll in the city during 1349 is unknown but may have approached 2,500 (two-fifths of the population) and at least half of its clergy. Four churches were closed through lack of parishioners. Shops and market stalls were left empty and fell into ruin. There were further outbreaks in 1361–2 and 1369, after which the churchyard of St Peter Mancroft had to be extended into what had been the cloth market. St Winwaloy's parish (by Surrey Street) was almost deserted as a result of the plague.

Part of the blame for the epidemics was put on poor sanitation and efforts were made (largely unsuccessfully) to clean up the city. In 1375 Adam de Hindringham, a barber, was accused that he 'is wont constantly to lay his muck in the King's highway through the whole year and likewise his carts by day and night to the great nuisance of the neighbours and of all that gather together there, whereby the said way is always deeply and foully encumbered.' He was fined 12*d*. In 1380 all muck or refuse in the market-place was ordered to be removed within four days. Complaints continued and in 1467 everyone in the city 'poor people however oppressed with want excepted' were ordered to heap up all of the filth that had gathered beside their house into the middle of the street and then cart it away. Further, when the streets had dried up they were to be levelled up with sand or stone. The dumping of refuse and waste from the industries along the riverside had also made the Wensum a serious health hazard – especially for those who relied on it for drinking water. In 1422 the Corporation ordered the cleaning of the river: from Calkmill to Bishop Gate was to be cleaned by those men living in Ultra Aquam and from Bishopgate to Thorpe by the rest (Conesford, Mancroft and Wymer wards). They were to work from 5 a.m. to 7 p.m. but could pay 4*d* a day for a labourer to take their place.

Pettus House on Elm Hill was the only medieval house within the street that survived the fire of 1507. It is a small merchant's house of the fifteenth century, with the jettied first floor carried on ground-floor walls of flint rubble

There were other hazards in walking around the city. In 1354 it had to be ordered that:

boars, sows and pigs before this time have gone and still go vagrant by day and night without a keeper in the said city, whereby divers persons and children have thus been hurt by boars, children killed and eaten, and others [when] buried exhumed, and others maimed, and many persons of the said city have received great injuries as wrecking of houses, destruction of gardens of divers persons by such kind of pigs.

Pigs were to be kept penned with the exception of Saturday afternoons whilst the sties were cleaned out.

The effects of disease on the total population of the city were mitigated by continued immigration from the countryside to serve the growing textile industry. In 1353 Norwich was made one of the ten staples in England for the trade of wool, leather and lead. Henceforth, these goods had to be brought here to be weighed and subjected to customs dues. There were again about six thousand people in the city by 1377. By this time Norwich was the principal place of manufacture for worsted (a fine cloth woven from long-staple wool fibres) while the later statutes of 1444 and 1467 empowered the Norwich Worsted Weavers' Guild to regulate the industry throughout East Anglia. From the fifteenth century Dornix cloth (made from linen thread and short wool fibres) also became very popular for bed curtains, wall-hangings and other covers.

Civic Wealth

The committee of twenty-four prominent citizens (soon to be known as aldermen, if not already) to assist the bailiffs in governing the city became increasingly more important. A charter of 1380 gave them and the bailiffs the power to make and alter by-laws. Their position was then consolidated in new charters of 1404 and 1417 which formally established the rule of mayor and two sheriffs (to replace the bailiffs), the committee of twenty-four aldermen and sixty-four common councillors. The charter of 1404 also created Norwich as a county in its own right. To suit its new status, the council was to be accompanied by appropriate pomp, with the mayor entitled to have a sword carried before him and be accompanied by sergeants carrying gilt maces bearing the royal arms. William Appleyard was the first mayor and Robert Brasyer and John Dannard the first two sheriffs. This centralization of power into the hands of a merchant clique resulted in some resentment from the wider body of freemen who claimed it had been achieved without seeking their consent.

Local government now had much wider functions. The council tried to intensify control of trade by bringing it directly into their hands rather than simply trying to regulate it. They bought up vacant market stalls and in 1379 acquired the common staithe off King Street, ordering all boats to unload there. In 1384 they obtained the property between Pottergate and the market to make the south part a common inn and the part fronting Pottergate a sale hall – the Worsted Seld.

The fifteenth-century Old Barge on King Street was originally intended to serve partly as a warehouse and partly as a display hall. In the latter half, one spandrel of the arch-braced, queen post roof is decorated with a carving of a dragon with a foliated tail. The building was converted to domestic use *c.* 1468

Anyone wishing to sell their cloth in the city had now to come here. Craft guilds were also more integrated into local government, and guild officials had to be presented to the mayor for approval. The city also took a half share of the fines that the guilds imposed for poor work. Despite the recent plague, this is all evidence of a town alive – not dying.

An increasing civic wealth and pride is seen in the construction of new municipal buildings. The Cow Tower beside the Wensum was rebuilt during 1399–1430. The market cross was rebuilt in 1409, the Murage Loft in 1411, the Guildhall in 1407 and the New Mills by 1429. The Guildhall, on the north side of the market-place, was built to symbolize the new powers vested in the city by its Charter of Incorporation in 1404. It was the largest medieval city hall built outside London. A contemporary account shows how the building work was ruthlessly pushed forwards: members of the Assembly were empowered to press carpenters, carters and workmen into service from

Norwich Guildhall, dating from 1407–53 is the largest medieval city hall outside London. It is built of flint rubble, faced with carefully knapped and galleted flint. The upper part of the gable has a decoration of lozenge and triangular chequerwork, made up of opposed flint and freestone

5 a.m. to 8 p.m. as needed. A tax was imposed on the citizens to finance the work. The cells built in the undercroft were opened in 1412 but it was not until 1453 that the building was finally completed. There were dungeons in the undercroft (a survivor of the earlier toll-house on the site), on the ground floor was a large open prison divided for men and women, on the first were two halls used for council proceedings and as courtrooms together with a guest chamber. The two-storey porch had a chapel beside it.

Although the Guildhall now stands in splendid majesty, during the middle ages it would have been surrounded by market stalls, with the scribes having lead-covered booths against the east gable wall. Here they would write out for the citizens the accounts, letters, petitions and so on that were needed for the business that took place within. Just downhill from the Guildhall was the pillory used in the punishment of minor offences.

Urban Poverty

It is generally believed that there was a decline in the city's economic fortunes during the fifteenth century. It is therefore ironic that some of Norwich's finest monuments date from this period. For while the poor may have been getting poorer and more widely distributed, many of the ruling clique were getting richer. The prosperity of the few can be seen in the rebuilding of almost all of the churches from 1350 to 1530 by their patrons. Most notable of all was the complete rebuilding of St Peter Mancroft between 1430 and 1455. But underlying dissent bubbled to the surface. In 1381 Norwich had been forced to defend itself against Wat Tyler's revolt. One of his lieutenants, John the Litester (dyer), was a Norwich man and brought an army of rebels to camp outside the city. The citizens distributed weapons, closed the gates and tried to buy the rebels off. But it was to be to no avail and it is likely that many in the city actually sympathized with the rebels, who were able to enter the city and burn the houses of noblemen and lawyers. The city was eventually relieved by the bishop who had collected an army around him. There was also continued tension between the city and the Cathedral Priory which gave the excuse for riot. In 1443 'Gladman's Insurrection' took place. The mayor and commons were accused of trying to burn the houses of leading clerics – Thomas Browne, Bishop of Norwich, John, Abbot of Holme, and John Heverlond, Prior of Norwich – and saying 'let us burn the priory, and kill the prior and monks'. The dispute continued until 1534 when the prior finally relinquished claims to jurisdiction outside his precinct.

An idea of the atmosphere in the city around this time is given by the order of 1461 that shopkeepers should keep one stave per man servant 'for preserving the peace in the city, and for resisting rioters and rebels'.

But local events were overshadowed in the latter half of the fifteenth century by the Wars of the Roses which lasted from 1455 to 1485. The wars contributed significantly to a general decline in the city's fortunes in the latter half of the fifteenth century. They interrupted normal trade and led to a decline in the worsted industry by detaching it from its continental markets. The wars also brought additional expense as the city was forced to supply men and arms to both sides, including 120 men sent to Henry VI before the Battle of Northampton in July 1460, together with some food and plenty of ale. The citizens also had to pay for the repair of the defences, as in 1481. Fresh economic ventures were sought as a recompense but they failed. By 1486 there were no stall-holders for the new fairs established in 1482.

Yet this decline should not be overstated. The evidence from the archaeology is for a continuance of the steady pattern of house alteration and rebuilding roughly every forty years as seen in previous periods. Indeed there seems to have been a new intensity in the late fifteenth century. In part this rebuilding may have been given impetus by fires in 1412 and 1413 which destroyed a large part of the town (including Blackfriars). There was also evidence of continuing

St Peter Mancroft on Hay Hill is the market church of the city. It was completely rebuilt between 1430 and 1455 as an expression of the wealth of the city merchants. This view dates from the turn of the century

As well as the four main orders of friars, Norwich supported a host of other religious bodies. One community of religious women occupied the Beguinage at the top of Elm Hill. This dates to the fourteenth century (surviving the fire of 1507) and was known as 'Le Godes Hous'. It became the King's Head Inn but changed its name in 1804 to the Briton's Arms during the republican fervour following the French Revolution

small-scale speculation. One house excavated on Oak Street in 1977, was newly constructed in the late fifteenth century and had clearly been built as one structure but was designed to be subdivided into two single room units. It featured a shared cesspit attached to the rear wall which straddled the line of the partition. The fifteenth century also saw the construction of a large number of brick-vaulted undercrofts beneath more substantial buildings. Over sixty still survive and records of over another thirty are known. They provided a level platform with which to build out over a slope and also provided fireproof storage for trade goods. There is little evidence that they served any public function.

CHAPTER EIGHT

Early Tudor Norwich

T he arrival, with the victory of Henry VII at Bosworth, of the Tudor Age in Norwich was marked by an outbreak of the 'sweating sickness'. It was an inauspicious start to an age that was to bring sweeping changes to the city. The population of Norwich towards the end of the medieval period was around 10,000; by *c.* 1575 it was around 17,000. The massive increases in population of the sixteenth and later seventeenth century still left local variations in the density of occupation. Thus, despite the fact that the Landgable entries for the Botolph Street area suggest that the number of holdings may have doubled between 1490 and 1547, the archaeological evidence from excavations here, as elsewhere in the city, pointed not to new building but to the extension of existing buildings into yard areas. Large open spaces remained because there was presumably more

A row of early sixteenth-century cottages in Gildencroft, on the south side of St Augustine's churchyard. These represent the rare survival of poorer quality buildings with an original ground plan of two unheated rooms

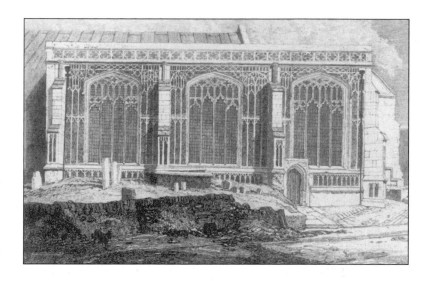

The trend of rebuilding the city's churches continued into the sixteenth century. St Michael Coslany was extended by Robert Thorp in the early sixteenth century, including the remarkable flushwork on the south aisle and chapel (that on the chancel is a careful nineteenth-century restoration). Such monuments were designed to be a show of prosperity – but at the same time the majority of the city's inhabitants were facing the consequences of an ever widening gulf between rich and poor. (*Engraving by J. Cotman*)

profit to be had from modifying existing properties than from building new ones.

Rich and Poor

The gulf between the small number of wealthy families in the city and the bulk of the population was growing wider during the sixteenth century. Fewer than thirty of the city's wealthiest citizens controlled over 40 per cent of Norwich's wealth. The city built an ornate council chamber in the Guildhall in 1535, and wealthy merchants such as Robert Jannys (mayor in 1517 and 1524) could afford a Flemish terracotta tombchest in St George Colegate; Nicholas Sotherton could rebuild Strangers Hall and furnish it with Flemish tapestries; and Robert Thorp could erect and endow the Thorp chantry chapel in St Michael Coslany. By contrast, the market-place was overgrown with weeds in 1544 and by 1570 the poor were sleeping in 'Barns and hay chambers'. The worsted trade was collapsing and weavers were leaving the city to avoid city rates. To try to halt this in 1524, it was ordered that all worsted cloth should be finished in Norwich wherever it had actually been woven. In 1542 Henry VIII ordered that no one could buy worsted yarn unless it was for weaving in Norwich or Norfolk. But even wool from the cathedral flock was being smuggled out of the country in order to sell to the rival Flemish industry.

This is the context for the support of many in the city for Kett's rebellion in June/August 1549. Robert Kett was a yeoman farmer and tanner who sympathized with local peasants in their objections to enclosures around Hethersett. Their protests widened and eventually a rebel army of 20,000 was camped on Mousehold Heath. Many in the city supported the rebels against the landlords who were extending the sheep pastures and threatening labourers' employment. Hopes were raised when Kett defeated the Earl of Northampton's forces in a battle around St Martin-at-Palace Plain on 1 August. Considerable damage was done in the process – Bishop Bridge gate was damaged and Whitefriars Bridge demolished; buildings at the Great Hospital and on the Common Staithe were destroyed. Kett, however, was defeated by the Earl of Warwick on 25 August. The fact that a number of market stalls remained vacant after the rebellion suggests that several of the stall-holders may have joined the rebels, and were either executed among the forty-eight hanged in the city or had fled. Kett himself was hanged from the walls of the castle. Sympathy for the rebels remained and some passers-by from the neighbouring countryside who looked up and saw the body swinging there expressed the wish that the king and council would allow the remains to be taken down and not 'hanged up for winter store'.

Fortunately, the effects of the decline of worsted weaving on what had been the mainstay of the city economy may well have been mitigated by the building of a reputation for other types of high quality worsteds such as sayes and camblets used for gowns and bed-hangings. There is a tale of envy from fashion-conscious sixteenth-century Norwich. John Drakes, a shoemaker, wanted a gown *exactly* like one being made up for Sir Philip Calthorp of St Martin-at-Palace Plain. Sir Philip heard of this and therefore ordered the tailor to cut holes in his (and therefore also in John Drake's). When Drake saw the result he exclaimed: 'by my latchet, I will never weare gentleman's fashion againe.' By no means everyone was involved in the textile industry. In 1535 the figure stood at only 30 per cent, but people employed in this way were the principal providers of the wealth that supported the other sectors of the city economy. There was also a rise in the importance of the distributive trade – mercers, grocers and drapers. Those involved in other manufacturing industries, leather, metalwork and the building trade, were generally among the poorest of the city.

Changes in the City

A series of disastrous fires in the early sixteenth century provided a watershed for building history. There was a fire in 1502 which swept westwards from Tombland through to St Andrew's. In 1505 another fire broke out north of the river in Colegate and burned for two days,

Bridewell Alley looking towards St Andrew's church. This is second in size only to St Peter Mancroft. It was one of many of the city's churches that was rebuilt in the late fifteenth and early sixteenth century. Norwich still maintains much of the atmosphere of narrow medieval streets

Copper alloy pilgrim's sign dating to the late fifteenth/early sixteenth century. It is made of two disks set in a wirework frame with two glass beads. One side (illustrated) has a decoration of Virgin and Child while the other shows St George and the Dragon. Its method of construction shows Low Countries influence

A row of late fifteenth-century houses on Pottergate was destroyed during the 1507 fire. The floors collapsed into the cellars beneath, which were abandoned and backfilled soon afterwards. As a result, excavation in 1973 was able to recover a remarkable collection of early sixteenth-century kitchen utensils

Late fifteenth/early sixteenth-century skillet made of copper alloy and found in one of the Pottergate cellars. Height 16.8 cm

spreading into Coslany. In 1507, there were two fires: 718 houses south of the river were burned down in four days in March 1507, while on 4 June a second fire broke out north of the river which lasted for two days, destroying another 360 houses. As a consequence, 40 per cent of the city's housing stock was destroyed. In 1509 Assembly ordered that in future 'all buildings within the City which shall be rebuilt anew shall be covered with thaktyle [tile] and by no means with reed straw called thakke [thatch] under penalty of 20s for every offence of every house or building detected' (but in 1570 there were still complaints about the presence of thatched houses). Many of the sites remained derelict until at least 1534, when the city obtained powers to compel owners to rebuild their houses or at least to enclose the land with a wall. Again, this was not immediately successful and in 1538 there were complaints that refuse was being dumped in vacant land near Prince Inn.

The order of 1570 gave particular warnings about the negligence of neighbours and the dangers of the wind carrying sparks across the city 'whiche sodenly kybdell [kindle] and overpasse beyonde all expectacion'. It also provided detailed instructions on dealing with fires. There were to be new fines for those who did not roof with tile or lead, the money going towards the cost of fire-buckets and ladders. The churchwardens were also instructed to ensure that they had sufficient buckets and a ladder at their churches, while each alderman was to have in his house twelve buckets and one ladder. All the buckets were to be marked to prevent theft. Each ward was also to have one 'crome' (hook) and four great ladders. Buckets were also to be provided beside every common well. Carriers and brewers had to be ready to carry water to the point of any fire, the signal being a backwards peal of bells. The only exception to the prohibition against thatch was if a roof adjoined by thatch on each side had to be repaired. Chimneys were also required to be properly swept and firebacks made good.

The tradition of clay-walled buildings, associated with fire-prone thatched roofs, came to an abrupt end in the aftermath of the fires of 1507. These precipitated both a widespread rebuilding programme and an extension of building types – evident from the Sanctuary Map of 1541. Houses were now almost exclusively constructed with ground floors of flint-and-brick rubble, a development which already had begun to filter down the social scale in the fifteenth century. Although building materials changed, the two-room ground plans for poorer houses continued, with an increase in complexity of plan and possible greater room specialization only coming in the later sixteenth century.

Elm Hill was almost completely destroyed during the fire of 1507 but, in contrast to other parts of the city, was largely rebuilt by about 1530. It has provided sixteen mayors or sheriffs of the city

One notable change, however, was the introduction of built fireplaces into the plan. The chimneys of these are clearly visible in the 1541 Sanctuary Map.

Apart from the fires the other events that brought dramatic changes to the city were the church reforms of 1535–6 and the dissolution of the monasteries between 1538 and 1548. Around a quarter of the city changed ownership, and only the lands of the cathedral and the Great Hospital remained intact. Much of the open land within the former friary precincts remained thus, however, until the eighteenth century and later. A religious connection was maintained as many of the new non-conformist chapels of the eighteenth century were built within their former bounds. In the nineteenth century they still represented the largest areas of available space, so were used for the new factories (such as the Yarn Mill on Whitefriars and brewery on Austin Friary). Three of the precincts were taken over by wealthy families to provide town houses and gardens: St Mary in the Field by the Hobarts, Austin Friars by the Howards and the nunnery at Carrow by the Sheltons. The Whitefriars, Franciscan and Old Dominican sites passed into multiple ownership but remained undeveloped in large part. The new Dominican site south of the river was bought by the Corporation. Indeed, many of the former ecclesiastical buildings took on municipal functions which meant that no new purpose-built municipal buildings were constructed until the eighteenth century. The Blackfriars became

During restoration work on St James's church, Pockthorpe in 1979, the base of a possible pulpit or tomb was discovered broken up within the core of the chancel wall. The four faces are each decorated with the symbols of one of the four evangelists (the eagle of St John being illustrated). The base was probably broken up at the Reformation

an assembly hall, mint, school, cloth hall and then Dutch church. The chapel of Carnary College was used to house the grammar school in 1553 after it was moved from the Blackfriars. Some of the medieval hospitals (which were closed under the act abolishing chantries) were taken over by the Corporation and used as plague houses. The Great Hospital became an old folk's home with the chancel divided up into wards, so preserving the magnificent 'Eagle Roof'. The nave was still retained for worship. Seventeen parish churches were also lost during the period 1520–70. An act of 1536 allowed two adjacent parishes to be united and one of the churches dispensed with if they were less than a mile apart, and one was worth no more than £6 per year. Some of the churches were demolished but others found new uses. St Mary the Less was used as a sale hall for cloth before becoming a church for the French-speaking refugees. Demolition brought its own profit, and building materials from the demolished churches and other ecclesiastical sites were spread as rubble throughout the city.

Attempts to improve the city also continued. In 1517 a common tumbrel was provided out of public collection together with a channel raker whose job it was to collect the muck from the streets and cart it away weekly. Householders had to collect their refuse into round heaps away from the drain for it to be collected. It all seemed to be to little avail as in 1552 the streets were still declared to be 'fowle and fylthye'. Later, in 1570, scavengers were appointed for each parish to

No. 15 Bedford Street. This is a remarkable survival of an early sixteenth-century shop, complete with evidence of its front door and windows. Not visible is the barrel-vaulted brick undercroft that belonged to an earlier, fifteenth-century, building on the site

ensure the regulations were kept and 'All common dunghilles be utter-
ly prohibited and forbidden.' But the continued difficulties in enacting
new legislation suggest that the city was facing an uphill struggle
against the traditional practices of its inhabitants.

Norwich Underground

The increased use of flint rubble and lime mortar in buildings after
1507 demanded new sources of raw materials. While some flint
may still have been collected from the seashore, or mined with
chalk from open quarries, other supplies may have been mined
from directly beneath the city. Large parts of Norwich are built
over former chalk and flint mines. Some date back to at least the

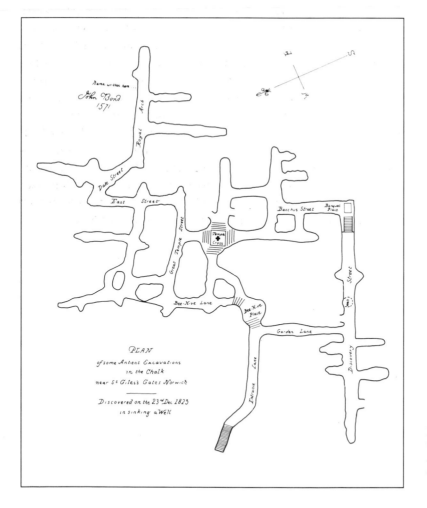

Plan of the Earlham Road
tunnels running adjacent to St
John's cathedral. The system
contains a piece of graffiti to
'John Bond 1571'

sixteenth century and those underneath Pottergate may even have a Saxon origin.

Evidence of mining, as well as open pits, has been found on all sides around Norwich, cut into the sides of the meandering valleys of the Rivers Yare and Wensum. Mine tunnels have been found around the outskirts of the medieval city and also within its bounds – on King Street/Ber Street and in the Pottergate/Westwick Street area. They can be as shallow as 3.6 m (11 ft) below the ground (Churchill Road) to over 27 m (80 ft) (Rosary Road), depending on the height of the valley side above them, and vary in height from 2 m to 4 m (6 ft to 12 ft). Where it has been possible to plan them, the pre-nineteenth-century tunnels have been cut horizontally into the hillside with the tunnels following a rough grid pattern. The best known are probably those running beneath the east end of Earlham Road, principally because a double decker bus collapsed into a tunnel during 1988! A plan drawn up of the 488 m (1,600 ft)-long system in 1823 shows a piece of graffiti to 'John Bond 1571'. It is impossible to be certain of their date, although those on the east side of the city (and including the open cast mines of Lollards Pit), may well have been used from the Norman period to provide building materials for the nearby cathedral and other buildings (including the 2^1/$_2$ miles of city walls from 1297) as well as quicklime for the tanning industry. The early name of Upper Goat Lane – Stonegate – may also reflect the pre-twelfth-century (and possibly Saxon) use of the mines running beneath there from an entrance off Westwick Street. It is likely, however, that their most intensive period of use was from the sixteenth century, when the use of flint increased rapidly and lime was also being used in agriculture.

CHAPTER NINE

The Strangers in Norwich

T he first contemporary view of Norwich comes from two maps of the mid-sixteenth century. The Cunningham Prospect of 1558 reflects a city of contrasts, with clusters of chimneyed two-storey buildings on the frontages and other buildings behind – but also with large open spaces, particularly to the east around the cathedral Close, in St Stephen's and in the north of the city. Beyond the walls there were only small suburbs at Heigham and Pockthorpe. The more sketchy Sanctuary Map of 1541 shows the same pattern but with more detailed views of one of these courtyard developments. Archaeology has added to the picture by showing how such buildings might have been subdivided to provide an even more cramped housing environment.

This was a time of enormous contrasts in wealth. In 1571 the poor in Norwich were estimated to be 2,300 persons, over half crowded into west Wymer ward and north of the river, and almost a quarter being textile workers. They lived in church porches, cellars, doorways, barns, hay chambers and other vermin ridden 'back corners'. Begging was banned and a workhouse was established at the Norman's Hospital for the men to grind malt and the women to spin and card wool. It was to house twelve poor folk who would only be fed if they worked, with hours running from 5 a.m. to 8 p.m. in the summer. There was a half hour meal break and a quarter hour break for prayers.

Disease thrived in such conditions. The plague of 1578–9 may have killed up to a third of the population of the city. There were further outbreaks in 1583–6, 1590–3 and regularly during the first half of the seventeenth century. There was little the city could do against the plague except try to limit contact. In 1579 it was ordered that no one should leave an infected house for six weeks. No one was to go out who had any sores. In 1580 no one was to leave an infected house until the plague had ceased there for at least twenty

Part of the Sanctuary Map of 1541. This shows St Stephen's church at the top of the picture with a courtyard development below it. On the street frontage is a two-storey building with single-storey cottages behind. Also shown is St Peter Mancroft church, the Guildhall and the market cross. The chimneys shown on the houses reflect the widespread introduction of built fireplaces after the fires of 1507

The Cunningham Prospect of 1558 shows the same pattern of housing as depicted on the Sanctuary Map, but the contrast between areas of dense housing and open space is more evident. Note also the absence of any large-scale development outside the city walls, except for the small suburbs in Heigham and Pockthorpe

days, unless carrying a 2 ft long white stick. A notice with 'Lorde haue mercye upon us' was to be posted on the door of any infected house and was to remain there for a month after the infection ceased. Prisons were set up to restrain those who would not comply. By the seventeenth century the realization of the hazards of poor sanitation meant that cesspits were no longer built into houses, but were pushed out to the bottom of the yard. Attempts were also made to improve the water supply, the poor quality of which did, however, remain a significant factor in spreading disease into the nineteenth century. But in 1577 the city did receive its first pumped water supply. It was thought that the disease might be passed from animals and an order was passed in 1630 to kill and bury any dogs, cats, pigs and tame doves that were found wandering the streets. There was little medical treatment available but the Dutch community appointed Peter Heybaud to look after their infected, so he and his family were ordered to carry a red stick, a yard and a half long, when out in public as a warning sign and not to go out after dark unless absolutely necessary. Searchers were also appointed to check the dead for the characteristic sores ('God's Tokens') before any were concealed in shrouds.

Rich and poor still lived cheek by jowl but attitudes were changing. There was a complaint in 1563 that some old houses bought by John Thurston were to be pulled down rather than be repaired, but another said: 'God forbid for what would the people say, then that they would say that gentlemen came to the City to buy up the houses and to pull down poor folks' houses to the intent that they would not have poor people to dwell near unto them.' The widening range of house types from the late sixteenth century – as reflected in both documents and archaeology – suggests a more complex social stratification. Increasing room specialization is typically reflected on sites by the addition of a further room (often cellared) to the plan.

In spite of the outbreaks of plague, by the 1620s the population was *c.* 20,000 and by the end of the seventeenth century it had reached around 30,000. Although there was a rising trend in population generally and an increasing proportion was living in the towns, to a large degree the city was rescued by massive immigration. Norwich had a long tradition of both trade and immigration from the continent which extended back into the Saxon period. By 1378, the number of Flemish weavers was so great that the citizens petitioned parliament to prevent 'the strangers', as they were called, from buying or selling merchandise. In 1495 two Dutchmen – Peter Peterson and Gerard Jonson – were sworn as citizens for 5 marks each.

A new era in Norwich's history, however, was heralded in 1554 when the merchant Thomas Marsham persuaded a dozen weavers from the Netherlands to settle in the city in order to manufacture the russells and sateens which were threatening the traditional worsteds. This experiment with the russell weavers led to more extensive attempts to officially encourage immigration. Religious persecution in the Low Countries from 1565 caused a widespread immigration of Protestant refugees to England. The city fathers of Norwich sought to take advantage of this, and the mayor, Thomas Sotherton, invited twenty-four Dutch and six Walloon (French-speaking Belgian) master weavers to the city in 1565 in order to revive the flagging textile industry and for the 'help, repair and amendment of our city of Norwich'. Others followed and by 1583 there were 4,679 Dutch and Walloons in the city, comprising a third of the population of the city. The rise in numbers would have been even more dramatic had not a

Tin-glazed earthenware jug made in Antwerp in the early to mid-sixteenth century. The central polychrome design is of the common religious monogram – IHS. It was found on Princes Street in 1973. Height 12.6 cm

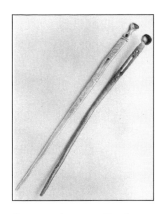

Seventeenth-century Dutch head-dress pin, dated to the seventeenth century, found in Norfolk. That on the right is from Market Avenue, Norwich, and is made of copper alloy (129 cm long). That on the left is from Aslackton, and is made of silver

further 2,500 died of the plague in 1578–9. By the early seventeenth century there were over 6,500.

The immigrants met a mixed reaction. In 1569 the mayor and aldermen wrote to the Privy Council stating that the 2,866 Strangers 'do lyve in good quiete and order, and that they traveyle diligently to earne their lyvings'. In 1567 the hatmaker, Claus van Werveken, had written home to his wife in Antwerp: 'You would never believe how friendly the people are together, and the English quite loving to our nation.' They were given considerable incentives including being allowed to lease redundant churches for their own use: the bishop's chapel was used by the Walloons from 1566 to 1637; Blackfriars Hall was used as the Dutch church from 1596, after temporarily serving as the cloth hall. St Mary the Less, also used at first as a cloth hall (from 1623), became the church of the Walloons from 1637. Some resentment was, however, inevitable and in 1570 a number of the local gentry claimed that the immigrants were threatening English livelihoods, and called upon the citizens to 'put the Strangers out of the City of Norwich'. Fortunately this call met with little response but their activities were strictly regulated in order to protect native trades. Tailors, butchers, shoemakers or cobblers, for instance, had to screen their shop windows with a 3 ft high lattice and could only work for, and sell to, other aliens. There was an 8 p.m. curfew and they could not buy wool in the market before midday. By 1579 they were being widely accused of spreading the plague by the 'corrupte kepinge of their howses and necessaries [privies], and also for the great annoyance of the river by skowring their bays and wasshinge them all alongeste the ryver to the great infeccion of the same'. The plague did hit them very hard, partly because of the crowded conditions that they, as some of the poorest in the city, were forced to live in. Their death rate as compared to the native population was 3:1. Nevertheless, in 1583 the mayor and aldermen wrote to the Privy Council detailing how the immigrants had benefited the city, notably in rebuilding ruinous houses and setting the poor to work. The restrictions were removed in 1598 when they were admitted as freemen for the first time.

Most of the immigrants were weavers or were otherwise connected with the textile trade, making the light cloths of the 'New Draperies' – the Dutch making woollen cloths while the Walloons made the finer cloths. But their contribution to the local economy was much wider. The first printing press in the city was introduced in 1570 by Anthony de Soleme, a Fleming wine merchant admitted as a citizen in that year. Some, such as George Fenne, Valentine Isborne and Zachary Shulte, played a major role in the revitalization of the silversmithing industry, while others worked in the building industry or as brewers, bakers, lime-burners, potters, wood-turners, pin-makers, printers, farmers and gardeners. The work of the latter was described in 1575 as: 'they digge and delve a nomber of acres of grounde and do sowe flax . . . they dig and delve a grete quantite of grounde for rootes which is a grete succor and sustenaunce for the pore.' Thomas Fuller in 1662 observed that it was the Dutch who first 'advanced the use and reputation of flowers in this city'. But not all of the immigrants were successful: in 1630 John Wetinge asked to be allowed to return to Holland, having been committed to the bridewell.

Beer was a longstanding Dutch import, indeed described in 1542 as 'fit only for a Dutchman'. One of the complaints against the Strangers was for their readiness to set up local breweries so that 'dyvers and sundrie fforreners coming and resorting to inhabitt w'thin the same cittie (yf they be hable to buye x combe of mawlt, im'edyately after their entrie into the cittie), do sett upp brewing of ale and bere and retail the same agein etc.'

Men might change their trade as opportunity dictated. An insight into just one family comes from the letter of Giles Navegeer to his grandmother in 1569. He had arrived in Norwich in 1567, and had learnt book-binding for six months but gave it up as providing too little profit. He then worked in the brewery of his brother-in-law (Peter Bake of Ypres). Meanwhile his brother was learning a trade as a cutler, his father worked in a threadtwist factory, while his mother did outwork and his sister spun thread.

Despite the complaints of 1570, the Strangers quickly passed on their skills to benefit native workers. In 1576 Richard Whittell of Ringsale, Norfolk, apprenticed one son to the 'bayweuer' Charles Droghbroot and another to the pinner, Nicholas Vanbuston. Another Dutch pin-maker, Nicholas Beoscom, was provided with a house at St Giles Hospital in 1581 so that he could teach the children 'his science of makyng pynnes'.

Physical trace of their presence is now hard to find. A small group of buildings, such as the much restored row Nos 56–60 King Street, the Manor House in Bracondale or the Adam and Eve public house on Bishopgate, have the characteristic 'Dutch gables' which *may* be a reflection of Dutch or Flemish builders, although the degree of direct influence is not clear. Many of the bricks were, however, imported from the Low Countries. The only direct statement of a Dutch building is in 1630 when the Dutch were allowed to demolish 'the howse by them builded for a pesthowse'. Identified items of Low Countries manufacture of the sixteenth/seventeenth century are very few,

The most visible reminders of the Dutch influence in the city today are the surviving examples of Dutch gables, although it is not clear how many were actually built by Dutch workers. This is the seventeenth-century Adam and Eve on Bishopgate

Norwich excavations and watching briefs on building sites have produced large quantities of seventeenth-century imported pottery from the Low Countries. Some may have been imported as trade goods but other examples may have been the possessions of the Strangers. Above is a Werra dish from the Rhineland with a date of 1625, and below a North Holland slipware cockerel bowl dated 1614

although excavation has revealed possible Dutch head-dress pins from a number of sites. The most widespread sign of Low Countries influence in the city is from the pottery, which was imported into Norwich from a wide range of sources in north-west Europe throughout the medieval and post-medieval periods. Consequently, the city has some of the most important groups of late sixteenth- and seventeenth-century imported pottery from the Low Countries found in this country. In all, around 40 per cent of archaeological sites in the city have produced Low Countries/Dutch imports. A number of Strangers were involved in the pottery trade. In 1585 Charles Vanverkyn imported 'a Maund with pottes' valued at £6 2s 4d. In 1586 Peter Peterson, Alien, imported 300 'earthen pottes and pannes ratyd at £4' while Peter Hughbert brought in 'A small baskett of earthen pottes ratyd at 10s'. In 1595 Jaques Dehem imported a 'maunde of warming pannes valued £6'. Some pottery may have been made locally by immigrants. Two immigrants from Antwerp, Jaspar Andries and Jacob Janson, are believed to have had a delftware pottery on Ber Street between 1567 and 1571 where they 'followed their trade, making Gally Paving Tiles, and Vessels for Apothecaries and others, very artificially'.

It is important to differentiate, however, between a general indication of the social or commercial influence of the Low Countries in the city by virtue of its trading contacts, and what actually constitutes evidence of immigrant occupation in a specific building. This has led, at times, to some confusion over how the quantity of Low Countries pottery in the city might be interpreted. For instance, the large collection of seventeenth-century 'Anglo-Netherlands' drug jars found on a watching brief on London Street are important for what they tell us about commercial contacts, but were the sales goods of an English apothecary and *not* the possessions of an immigrant. The very large quantity of pottery imported as trade items, including the Rhenish stoneware drinking vessels that became ubiquitous on occupation sites of both native and immigrant, masks those properties that might have been occupied by the Strangers themselves. The clearest guide comes from the plainer slipwares and unglazed wares which occur on less than 8 per cent of sites, and which may well reflect actual Stranger households. But some of the highest quality wares may also have been the prized possessions of otherwise poor immigrants who had brought their decorated plates from their homeland. Large collections of Werra and North Holland slipwares and Dutch tin-glazed earthenwares were found in cesspits behind a subdivided property on Botolph Street in 1975. Ironically, both these and other finds from cesspits on Alms Lane occur in contexts that may well represent the abandonment of the properties by their immigrant tenants in the mid to late seventeenth century as they returned to their homelands. The immigrants did have different methods of cooking that demanded different types of vessel from those used by the natives of Norwich, and this might be expected to give a clue as to who was living on a property – but many of these were wooden and have long perished. Claus van Werveken wrote back to his wife in 1567 asking her to 'bring a dough trough for there are none here. . . . Buy two little wooden dishes to make up half pounds of butter: for all Netherlanders and Flemings make their own, for here it is all pig's fat.'

Despite the wealth that they brought to the city, the refugees were among the poorest in the city, mainly crowded north of the River Wensum, in the principal textile working district which was already one of the poorest areas of the city. In 1587, the Elders of the Dutch church complained that their congregation was too poor to pay the poor-relief payments and the city awarded them £10 to alleviate the distress. Their status meant that their houses were not of the standard that one would expect to survive. As a consequence, the absence of reliable diagnostic material has allowed us to identify confidently only five excavation sites as definitely containing the homes of the immigrants. The two sites where the evidence has been best preserved are in Alms Lane and Botolph Street, both in the textile working district of *Ultra Aquam*. The Alms Lane site was, indeed, owned by wealthy master-weavers for much of its history and its earliest documented tenant was the Walloon weaver, Jacob Votier, in 1725. Large quantities of Low Countries pottery and some fragments of Dutch decorated clay pipes were found on tenements within these sites. Until the early seventeenth century the houses here were relatively comfortable: there was little pressure on land in these outer areas and the buildings tended to have large ground plans. But *c.* 1600 the three houses on the Alms Lane and St George's Street frontages of the Alms Lane site were each subdivided to form a ground plan of one single room with one double-roomed unit. A similar pattern of subdivision, but on a higher-quality scale, was revealed on Botolph Street where a tenement was rebuilt *c.* 1625 as two units each of three rooms, and with the rear house possibly incorporating an industrial function. It is likely that the decrease in floor area as suggested by the archaeological plans was met by an increased use of upper storeys, and especially attic space, to provide the characteristic late seventeenth-century artisan's cottage of three storeys, including a continuous line of dormers lighting the attic workshop.

A characteristic bulk find from seventeenth-century sites in the city is clay pipes. It is unlikely that these were traded in any quantity from the Low Countries during the seventeenth century. Some decorated pipes may, however, have been brought over and have survived as keepsakes, such as the fragments of seventeenth-century decorated clay pipe stems from the Netherlands found in the backfill of a seventeenth-century rubbish pit on Alms Lane

Opposite: A comparison between the density of housing on fifteenth-century Alms Lane and that of the mid-seventeenth century shows how the massive immigration was dealt with by the intense development of existing properties rather than by expanding on to the open space that still existed in other parts of the city. As here, houses were subdivided and greater use was made of attic space to compensate

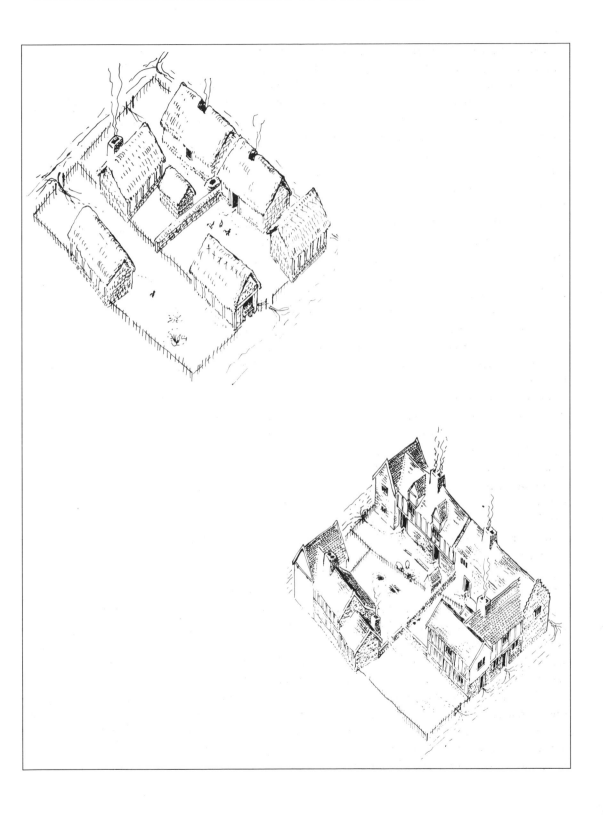

Similar evidence of subdivision of this period has been found on a number of other excavation sites. Documentary evidence points to even substantial houses being subdivided in this way – one of the largest accommodated eleven families. This would appear to have been the most common way in which the city coped with the population explosion of the late sixteenth/seventeenth century. This evidence for the creation of smaller housing units gels with the small number of surviving single-cell buildings that were newly built as such (as Nos 2–4 Lion and Castle Yard on Timberhill). New cottages were also built around courtyards during the sixteenth/seventeenth century, like the properties excavated on Oak Street. It is likely that a high percentage of such buildings were occupied by Strangers – especially north of the Wensum – even though no diagnostic evidence has survived.

By 1650 the number of Strangers had fallen to about a thousand. This was due partly to the repressive policies of Archbishop Laud to encourage repatriation, and later to the effects of the Dutch wars during the Commonwealth period. But the immigrants can fairly claim to have rescued the economy of Norwich from disaster, and the techniques that they had introduced became the basis of the New Draperies upon which the future textile trade came to depend.

A range of buildings excavated on Botolph Street in 1975. A quite substantial house was subdivided in the seventeenth century to provide a row of smaller cottages. These were served by a cess pit at the end of the narrow side yard. The quantity of Dutch pottery found in this cesspit suggests that the cottages were occupied by immigrants

Nos 2–4 Lion and Castle Yard, Timberhill are further examples of the diminishing resource of information about artisan life in the late sixteenth/seventeenth centuries. Like William Watson's house (p. 81), these are also rare examples of single-room plan cottages

CHAPTER TEN

Civil War and later

T he plague of 1625–6 left 1,431 dead and caused a doubling of the poor rate, but natural disasters of the seventeenth century were accompanied by political and religious conflict that ultimately culminated in civil war. King Charles tried to escape economic crisis by resorting to extra-parliamentary taxation such as Ship Money to support the navy and Coat and Conduct Money for the army, together with forced loans. The Crown also tried to restrict the tradition of nonconformist dissent in cities such as Norwich (most recently seen in the establishment of a number of puritan lectureships), a policy fuelled here by the appointment of one of Archbishop Laud's strongest supporters, Matthew Wren, as bishop. There were rising fears nationally of a Catholic conspiracy and in Norwich itself a supposed papist plot to burn down the city was discovered in November 1641 when, according to *Bloody Newes from Norwich* there was

> a great uproar in Norwich concerning the papists' arising there, they being intended to burn the whole city . . . one to begin at one end of the city, and the second at the other end, the one was discovered being about to set fire to a thatched house, the other he set the house on fire joining to High Bridge Street [Fyebridge Street], which was burnt to the ground, to the great astonishment of the whole city . . .

Norwich lay within an area that was basically loyal to Parliament, and conflict only took place around the fringes of Norfolk, notably at King's Lynn where, on 13 August 1643, the Governor declared for the king. But otherwise this was the heart of Cromwell's Eastern Association. The city's role during the Civil War was principally to supply troops and money to the parliamentary forces operating elsewhere in the region. Some work was carried out on the defences, mainly around the gates, but no evidence of this now survives and none has yet been recorded in archaeological excavations. But this

Cromwell's 'maiden troop'
depart from Norwich, 1643

effort should not be taken to suggest that the city was united in its
opposition to King Charles. The strongest support for Parliament within the council came from the poorer and industrial areas of Wymer and
north of the river, but Mancroft remained Royalist and the city continued to elect officers with known Royalist sympathies throughout the
war and Commonwealth period. At the end of 1643 a list was made of
432 Royalist suspects among the principal citizens.

As the battle lines began to be drawn up in 1642 Norwich, as elsewhere, was faced with conflicting demands from King and Parliament.
On 29 July, the Royalist Captain Moses Treswell arrived in the city to
levy 100 volunteers for the king's forces at Newark, but the Council
remained loyal to Parliament and Treswell was therefore arrested. In

preparation for any trouble the watch at the city gates was doubled and the gates locked at 9 p.m. All of the arms and powder were gathered together in the Armoury above the Assembly and the cannon was kept in the low room below the council chamber. It was now Parliament's turn to call upon the city to raise its militia and on 22 October there was a general muster of the trained bands and volunteers. Unfortunately there was a generally low opinion of such troops. They were described elsewhere as, although being 'the main support of the realm and its bulwark against unexpected invasion' they 'were effeminate in courage and incapable of discipline, because their whole course of life was alienated from warlike employment'.

The city feared an attack by loyal Royalist gentry who might be expected to command some loyalty from within the town and as a result an engineer, Mr Cristian, was brought from King's Lynn to advise on the fortifications of the city. Over £250 was spent on renewing the medieval defences; these had been designed for an age of warfare before cannon and would have been no match for a Civil War bombardment. Muskets and their bandoliers were bought, together with the still more gentlemanly pikes, and also crossbows. On 28 November earth was piled up ready to block the gates as earthen defences were far more effective than stone against cannon shot. Scouts were also sent out to warn of any impending attack. On 25 February 1643 Conesford gate was blocked and St Giles, Pockthorpe and St Augustine's gates locked. Discussions were also held about the construction of seven or twelve bastions and a breastwork against the river. Although there is no surviving plan, the intention was probably to create a star-shaped defence on the contemporary Dutch model. There was still no direct threat but 150 dragoons (mounted musketeers) were raised to send to Colonel Oliver Cromwell at Cambridge. The horses were at least partly seized from the property of Royalist sympathizers in the city.

It was now that the local Royalist party, which included the mayor, decided it was time to offer some resistance. The mayor, William Gostlin, refused to obey the order to seize Royalist arms and property and consequently, on 2 March 1643, he was seized in the Guildhall by the Parliamentarians and taken to Cambridge. There were clearly rumbles within the city at this action and on 10 March the watch was extended to guard the churches against the possibility of internal dissent. Some of the complaints would undoubtedly have been concerning the level of the weekly assessment for Norwich which Parliament had set at £53 to help support the war. Augustine Holl did try to organize some resistance and a number of conspirators met at his house, but they were foiled when Lieutenant Craske and his Norwich volunteers wheeled up the city cannon and threatened to use it to blow up the house – so they surrendered. Unfortunately, the next day a loaded cannon accidentally discharged, killing at least seventeen people. These incidents provided the excuse for the supporters of Parliament to carry out a purge of aldermen believed to be Royalist sympathizers.

More volunteers were raised on 13 and 26 March 1643. They were again used to reinforce garrisons elsewhere in the region. The young men and girls of Norwich also raised £240 to equip the 'Maiden Troop' of Cromwell's cavalry under Captain Robert Swallow which became the eleventh troop of the Ironsides. In early April it was feared that the then Parliamentarian King's Lynn was in danger of imminent attack, and so a company of volunteers under Sergeant Major Sherwood was sent there. Next they were asked to contribute towards the fortification of Cambridge. Men were also sent out to help garrison Wisbech and Lowestoft.

By July the threat seemed to be lessening and the gates were opened up again. But in August, with King's Lynn's defection to the king, the castle was being refortified, and the ditches were cleaned out. The war seemed to be getting closer. On 29 August a number of cannon were supplied to assist the siege of King's Lynn which had begun in that month. These consisted of two brass demi-culverins (4,800 lb), one of iron (3,400 lb), two falconets (600 lb) and two falcons (700 lb). King's Lynn surrendered to Parliament on 16 September, but already Norwich was being asked to contribute to campaigns further afield. On 11 September the aldermen sat at every church to collect whatever plate the citizens were prepared to give or lend to help pay Fairfax's army in the north: £516 5s was later raised towards the costs of retaking Newcastle. However, more people refused to contribute than those who actually did, including seven aldermen and over half of the members of the common council. In all, Norwich spent £3,543 8s on providing men and arms from 1 April to December 1643. At the same time, Norwich was also facing the consequences of other aspects of the Puritan ascendancy. Following an ordinance of August 1643 seeking the destruction of so-called monuments of idolatry and superstition, Aldermen Greenwood and Lindsey, assisted by one of the sheriffs, Thomas Toft, led a mob to sack the cathedral. Bishop Hall described the 'furious sacrilege': 'what clattering of glasses, what beating down of walls, what tearing down of monuments . . . what piping on the destroyed organ pipes . . . vestments . . . and the singing books and service books, were carried to the fire in the public market place . . . the cathedral was filled with musketeers, drinking and tobacconing, as freely as if it had turned alehouse'. Later in 1647, during the Commonwealth, lead was stripped from the bishop's palace and chapel, which were converted to houses for the poor. The citizens of Yarmouth wanted to go further and petitioned Parliament to give them 'lead and other useful materials of that vast and altogether useless Cathedral in Norwich' but fortunately Parliament refused.

More troops were sent to Cambridge in March 1644 but until the formation of the New Model Army it was generally difficult to persuade such local forces to fight elsewhere. Indeed, some of the Norwich officers refused to go and Captain Rayley resigned his commission. There are also the first reports of casualties of Norwich men as troops were killed at the siege of Newark by Prince Rupert. The survivors of the 'Norfolk Redcoats' appear to have lost much of their equipment as the Council had to provide a new sword for Captain Ashwell and a back, breast and helmet for Lieutenant Burton and Ensign Atteway.

Norwich then was caught up in the conflict between the Independents and Presbyterians which brought an uneasy alliance of the latter with Royalists and tradesmen in the city against the army and central government. In 1646 there were riots against excise duties, led by butchers. Royalists had been barred from holding office but Mancroft ward elected the known Royalist, Roger Mingay, as alderman in March 1648. The mayor, John Utting, allowed the election and a few days later permitted bonfires and feasting on the anniversary of Charles I's accession! He also resisted the orders for defacing monuments and for the reform of the clergy. On 18 April, therefore, he was ordered to be brought to the House of Commons to explain his actions. A mob tried to prevent this, threatening to hang the sheriff and ham-string anyone who interfered with the mayor. They set their own guards on the gates with the watchword 'For God and King Charles' while Utting's supporters on the council prevented any move to summon troops from the county. On 24 April, they raised 500 armed men in Chapel-Fields and then broke into the sheriff's house where weapons were stored (south side of St Michael at Plea) and plundered a number of other houses. Then they broke into the headquarters of the County Committee on Bethel Street where the magazine was. By now the Parliamentary forces in the surrounding countryside had been warned and Colonel Fleetwood arrived with eighty troopers. After a skirmish the rioters retreated to the Committee House on Bethel Street; unfortunately someone within was careless and ninety-eight barrels of gunpowder exploded, killing or injuring about a hundred people and damaging surrounding property, including Chapelfield House and the churches of St Peter Mancroft and St Stephen. The mayor surrendered the next day to avoid further trouble. One hundred and eight rioters were later prosecuted, of whom seven were executed by firing squad in the castle ditches.

Even though Norwich was outside the main area of actual fighting it found the Civil War to be a great strain on its fortunes. In 1649 the city petitioned Parliament to be relieved of some of their taxes because of the great loss and decay of trade caused by the war. In particular the war had disrupted the supply of yarn and the export of worsted cloth. Discontent continued and in October 1650 a plot was discovered for a rising in the city. Several were arrested and twenty-five were executed, but the freemen now began to undermine consistently the Parliamentary Corporation. Moderates and even Royalists were elected as aldermen, sheriffs and Members of Parliament.

Oliver Cromwell died in 1658 to be succeeded by the short-lived Protectorate of his son Richard. Many of the citizens of Norwich, including aldermen and common councillors, signed a petition to General Monk as he marched on London in January 1660 complaining of 'the miseries of an unnatural war, the too frequent interruptions of government, the imposition of several heavy taxes, and the loud outcries of undone and almost famished people, occasioned by the general decay in trade'. Norwich and Norfolk it seems, were well ready for the Restoration, as called for by the Convention Parliament

The cramped yards became a feature of post-medieval Norwich. This example is on King Street

This building (the Little Gallery) at the east end of Elm Hill shows the movement away from timber framing in the late seventeenth century and the greater use of brick in house construction. The brick string course is characteristic of 1690–1710

The best preserved example of a late seventeenth-century weaver's single-room plan cottage is William Watson's House, No. 63 St George's Street. Now much restored, it was dated by a plaque to 1670

on 1 May. King Charles II was solemnly proclaimed in the city on 10 May 1660 and a thanksgiving was held on 24 May. On 20 September, to the relief of all, the garrison was finally disbanded. One of the final local casualties of the war was Miles Corbett of Sprowston and MP for Yarmouth. He had signed Charles I's death warrant and was executed as a regicide.

Life then slowly returned to what passed for normal in the seventeenth century. There were further outbreaks of plague in 1662 and 1665; in the year from 3 October 1665, 2,251 of the inhabitants died of the plague in the city. Many shops were closed, the rich fled the city and there was mass unemployment. Fortunately famine was averted by a glut of herrings caught at Yarmouth!

It was now recognized what part improved sanitation played in helping to prevent the spread of disease. By the late seventeenth century pit digging to bury rubbish within the property had virtually ceased and there must have been a well organized (though largely undocumented) rubbish collection service. This movement was probably also spurred by the increasing enclosure and subdivision of yards, making access for the cleaning out of cesspits difficult. Much of the pattern of housing of the city during the sixteenth and seventeenth centuries had been one of adaption to the increased population pressure rather than new building and many of the existing houses were derelict by the late seventeenth century. This created a housing boom which now started for the first time to widely use brick rather than timber-framing. Writing even in 1698, however, Celia Fiennes could comment that the houses were 'of the old form, mostly in deep points and much tiling . . . their building timber and their plaster of laths . . . but none of bricks except some few beyond the river which are built of some of the rich factors like London buildings'. Many buildings were still thatched into the 1660s.

There were other improvements. The first fire engine was introduced to the city in 1668, no doubt spurred by tales from the Great Fire of London two years earlier as well as Norwich's earlier history. Efforts were also made to improve navigation for larger vessels on the Yare from the late seventeenth century. The Norwich and Yarmouth Navigation was formed in 1682 to impose duties on goods coming into Yarmouth with which to maintain and improve the artery of trade along the rivers (Yare, Bure and Waveney).

The Norwich textile industry expanded dramatically in the last quarter of the seventeenth century as the country cast off the sombreness of puritanism and took a new interest in fashion, eagerly buying up the

The Old Meeting House on
Colegate, built in 1693 for the
Independent congregation, is
one of the oldest and finest
meeting houses in the country.
The sash windows are reputed
to be the oldest in the city.
(*Engraving of a drawing by J.
Sillett*)

new silk mixture versions of more traditional cloths. Among the most
famous of the new 'Norwich stuffs' was 'Norwich Crape'. Celia
Fiennes could therefore write: 'The whole citty lookes like what it is, a
rich thriveing industrious place.' Nevertheless the industry, so vital to
the prosperity of Norwich, was already starting to feel the ill wind of
competition from the Indian calicoes and this trend was set to increase
in the following century.

CHAPTER ELEVEN

The myth of
Georgian elegance

'The walls of this city are reckoned three miles in circumference taking in more ground than the city of London; but much of that ground lying open in pasture, fields and gardens.' Thus did Daniel Defoe describe Norwich in the early eighteenth century. In one respect he was describing what was still very much a medieval town, defined by its thirteenth-century walls, and in terms of size it was still the second largest city in the country. But within the walls this was a very different looking city to medieval Norwich and although to Defoe it still presented an attractive open outlook (enhanced by the many fine buildings constructed during the late seventeenth and eighteenth centuries), this disguised the cramped squalor to be found in many parts of the city. There was not, however, the same massive rise of population as there had been in the preceding century, rising by only *c.* 7,000 during the century to *c.* 37,000 in 1801.

Norwich began the eighteenth century as the most important manufacturing centre outside London, but it lost this pre-eminence during the course of the century and faced increasing pressure on its all-important textile industry from the new centres in Lancashire and Yorkshire and from the import of cheaper Indian calicoes. In 1719 the city petitioned Parliament against such imports and also took more direct action. On 5 July according to the *Saturday Post* 'a Parcel of Fellows got together in a Mobbish Manner and tore People's Calico Gowns and Petticoats off their backs'.

Nevertheless, despite the problems of competition at home and abroad, it had managed to capture new European markets. Exports to Spain alone increased from £31,000 in 1711 to £112,000 in 1721. New markets were also found in Russia, India and China. Increasingly this trade was carried on direct from Norwich rather than relying on London middle-men. As a result, the mid-eighteenth century has been seen as the golden age of Norwich textile production producing a wide range of high quality fabrics – worsteds and worsted mixtures – and

Existing, but now unfashionable, timber-framed buildings might be concealed in the eighteenth century by a cladding of 'mathematical tiles' to give the impression of brickwork (Towler's Court, Elm Hill)

brightly coloured, with the quality of Norwich dyeing being equally renowned. But the industry increasingly depended on the fickleness of fashion for its luxury fabrics and never regained its stability. Manufacture was concentrated in small domestic workshops but the industry increasingly began to be dominated by a small number of firms who controlled most of the wealth. By the end of the century the worsted industry employed about ten thousand people directly or indirectly in Norwich and the surrounding countryside.

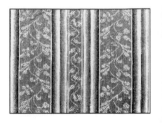

Norwich-made worsted clouded callimanco, dating from the late eighteenth century

Norwich also thrived on developments in local agriculture during the century, although the full potential was largely to be seen in the following century. Norfolk was an important producer of barley and malt and by the end of the eighteenth century there were several important breweries that were to develop further in the nineteenth century. In 1801 Patterson's brewery, only founded seven years earlier, was producing 20,000 barrels per year. Norwich was also an important cattle market: by the end of the century, following the levelling of the earthworks in 1738 and the filling of some of the ditches in 1774, most of the castle bailey was used as a cattle market while Horsham St Faiths had one of the largest cattle markets in early eighteenth-century England. This served as an obvious spur to the traditional leather industry of the city. Thus Norwich remained a centre of distribution of produce for its rich agricultural hinterland as it had done since Saxon times. A new sign of prosperity came in the

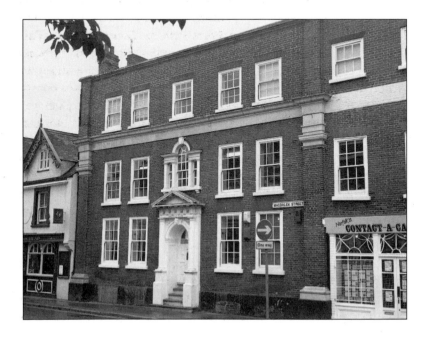

No. 44 Magdalen Street, with its Venetian window, is one of the most ornate Georgian houses in the city

mid-eighteenth century with the development of banking and insurance. In 1756 Charles Weston opened his bank in Norwich and the Gurney bank opened in 1775 (it still continues as part of Barclays). By 1782 they had branches at King's Lynn, Wisbech and Halesworth. The Norwich General Assurance Office was founded by Thomas Bignold in 1792 and the Norwich Union Fire Insurance Society soon after in 1797.

It was also a time of notable improvements to communications and therefore the prospects for trade. The river was significantly improved for larger craft and by the end of the eighteenth century more than half of the total output of the textile industry was being exported by river. The roads were also being improved. The process of turnpiking roads had begun at the very end of the seventeenth century but accelerated considerably from 1766, and this greatly improved the communication network around the city. The first regular coach service to London came in 1761. By 1783 there were eight coaches providing twenty-five departures weekly. There were a large number of carriers operating in the district around Norwich, providing a vital service in importing goods from the various rural outworkers who were still important: much of the spinning and carding of wool was still carried out in the villages.

Within the medieval walls, Norwich now looked very different – at least on the main street frontages. There are numerous surviving examples of the way in which the prosperity of the century was expressed in the new buildings of the city, whose quality is owed to the skills of notable local architects such as Thomas Ivory. This was first of all reflected in new public buildings: citizens were no longer prepared to make do with modifying the existing legacy of medieval Norwich. The Shire House was built in 1749 and a county gaol in 1792–3 on the castle mound. The Bethel lunatic asylum was built in 1714, a theatre in 1756, the Norfolk and Norwich Hospital in 1771–2 and a library in 1784. The finest of the Georgian buildings in the city is the Assembly House on Theatre Street, built in 1754 by Thomas Ivory. Crown building was represented by the cavalry barracks in Pockthorpe. As for domestic buildings, most of the medieval timber-framed buildings on the street frontages were now either rebuilt or were concealed behind brick façades with classical details. In some cases, thin tiles were hung on the front of the buildings to give the impression of brickwork (known as mathematical tiling). One of the best of the Georgian classically-designed buildings is Churchman House, No. 68 St Giles Street, built *c.* 1750 and comprising two storeys of seven bays; but also especially notable is

Nos 25–31 Surrey Street is a
well restored urban terrace,
built by Thomas Ivory in
1761–71

the elegant urban terrace built by Ivory (in 1761–71) between Nos 25
and 31 Surrey Street, and comprising a row of buildings with four
storeys and basements.

The strength of nonconformity (reflected in a material sense by the
Quaker banking tradition) is seen also in new meeting houses, many of
which were built within the areas once housing the medieval friaries.
At the end of the preceding century were built the Independent
Meeting House of 1693 and Friends Meeting House of 1699. In the
eighteenth century itself the Octagon chapel of 1754–6 on Colegate
and the Baptist chapel of 1745 on St Mary's Plain (now rebuilt), were
built. John Wesley admired Thomas Ivory's architecture in the
Octagon but questioned the need for such elegance in a chapel, writing
in his diary:

I was shewn Dr Taylor's New Meeting House probably the
most elegant one in all Europe. It is eight square, built of the
finest brick, with sixteen sash-windows below, as many above,
and eight sky-lights in the dome, which indeed are purely orna-
mental. The inside is finished in highest taste, and is as clean as
any nobleman's saloon. The communion-table is fine
mahogany, the very latches of the pew-doors are polished
brass. How can it be thought that the old coarse gospel should
find admission here?

Churchman House, St Giles Street is one of the finest Georgian houses in the city. It was built between 1725 and 1740 by Alderman Churchman, and later housed Norwich High School for Girls

View of inner side of St Martin's gate from an original sketch of 1720 by J. Kirkpatrick. The city gates were all demolished between 1791 and 1801 as part of the movement to 'improve' the city

The tradition of quiet and industrious nonconformity in the city was quite at odds with other elements of 'genteel' society of the period. The Bell Hotel was the meeting place of the Hell Fire Club whose hooligan members were 'gentlemen of principles inimical to government and with a determination to crush the Methodists'. John and Charles Wesley were both attacked by members when they preached in the city in 1754. Another society was the Bell Corporation which was founded in 1764 and was governed by the pillars of society – the mayor and other civic officers; but this was split by opinion on the French Revolution in 1793 and the establishment faction moved across to the Castle Inn.

The impression of Georgian Norwich as presented by the carefully-restored buildings of today gives only a distorted sample of the period. The streets were regularly cleaned by the end of the century but to modern eyes the town of narrow streets, many still unsurfaced and with no pavements, lit by oil lamps, would appear filthy. The problems were recognized and the gates through the city walls, now described as 'a nuisance, that smells rank in the nose of modern improvement!', were demolished between 1791 and 1801 in order to try to improve the standard of health by increasing the circulation of air. Possibly the aim was also just to add to the city's modernity. The founding of the Norfolk and Norwich Hospital in 1771 was another major advance in providing improved medical care for the city. Few at the time would have recognized the concept of Georgian 'elegance': it was a city of great contrasts between elegant mansions on the main streets and the continuation of sixteenth- and seventeenth-century slums behind them.

But for those with wealth, and despite the increasing pressures being put on the textile industry, and the accelerating growth of the northern industrial towns, the city ended the century in a confident mood, looking forward.

CHAPTER TWELVE

Nineteenth-Century Expansion

View of Norwich market-place
c. 1812, with St Peter Mancroft
in background. Note the ladies
selling their wares from 'peds',
a feature of Norwich market

T he population of the city had been almost static in the second half of the eighteenth century but more than doubled during the first half of the nineteenth century, from 36,909 in 1801 to 68,195 in 1851; in 1900 it was around 120,000. Many of these people were farm labourers seeking to escape abject poverty on the land. Such numbers could no longer be housed simply within the city walls and extensive suburbs began to develop around the city, particularly to the west: the population of the

Norwich contained twenty-seven breweries in 1836, taking advantage of the ample water supply and local production of high quality malting barley. Bullards Brewery on Westwick Street was built in 1868

old medieval suburb of Heigham rose from 842 in 1811 to nearly 6,000 in 1841.

At the start of the century the dominant industry was the worsted and the new mixed fibre industries, with the Norwich shawl industry achieving world renown, but leather-working was set to replace these as the dominant labour-intensive industry by the end of the century.

The century saw the development of a factory economy with the Silk Yarn Mill being built on Cowgate in 1834 (rebuilt in 1836–9) and the Albion Worsted Yarn Mill on King Street around the same time (now part of Read Woodrow Mills). Numerically, in 1838, 3,398 out of 4,054 looms were still in weavers' cottages rather than in larger workshops or factories, but the factory product now far outweighed that which could be produced by hand. The initial impact was probably most felt by the large number of outworkers who were involved in preparing the hand-spun yarn from the wool.

The five-storied Jarrolds Silk Mill on Whitefriars was built in 1836, and is one of the first examples of the mechanization of the textile industry in the city. It was intended to be sublet to individual manufacturers and contained sixty-five spinning frames and five hundred power looms. It later became a chocolate factory and is now a printing works

The disruption in the trading of worsted to its markets caused by the Revolutionary and Napoleonic wars ended in 1815, but this was a period of repeated boom and slump with little security. The extension of steam power into worsted production halted the long-term recession in the industry for a while and encouraged a further development into the quality hand-made market, of which the Norwich shawls and crapes became particularly famous. For a time, weavers in this part of the industry could earn up to £10 a week. The first steam-powered

The Norvic shoe factory on Colegate, built for the firm of Howlett and White in 1876. Sir George White was a noted local Baptist and Liberal. Christian charity extended to paying the strike pay of local workers during a dispute in 1897, when the union cheque was delayed

loom was introduced into Norwich in 1838 and this certainly caused great pressure on the hand weavers of the lower quality goods, many of whom were now having to work sixty hours a week to earn only 5*s* 6*d*. Wages were slashed to reduce production costs in the face of competition from Yorkshire machine-made worsted, and riots, strikes and pickets followed. Employment in the industry was rescued temporarily by the improvement of rapid communications brought by the railways after the middle of the century. This allowed the now-mechanized industry to expand somewhat, but the area did not have the natural advantages of Yorkshire in terms of water power or coal supplies for maintaining the steam-driven mills. By 1900, only about two thousand people were still engaged in the textile industry.

Norwich was fortunate that other industries, and the further development of services introduced in the preceding century such as banking and insurance, could help offset the decline in the textile industry. From the mid-nineteenth century, Norwich came once again to depend on leather rather than on cloth. The period saw the start of the rise of a large shoemaking industry: by 1900 there were over 7,500 boot and shoemakers in the city. This was the natural inheritor of large-scale weaving labour in the city and until *c.* 1840 most manufacturing was on a small scale, but by the 1860s the industry was organized through distribution offices which employed large numbers of outworkers (employing 800–900 shoemakers). Then came the invention of leather-sewing machines so that by the end of the century half of the workforce was actually working in factories. One of the most famous of the factories was Howlett and White on Colegate, founded in the 1850s.

Brewing was also to be very important to the economy of the city, serving the 505 public houses in existence in 1845 – but not as a large-scale employer. In 1836 there were twenty-seven breweries but this fell to twelve in 1858 and seven in 1875, as the larger concerns bought up the smaller operations. Bullards moved to the Anchor Brewery in 1868; Crawshaws Brewery was on St Stephen's Street, with Youngs and Burt on King Street. The latter amalgamated on the King Street site. The largest of the breweries was Steward and Patterson at Pockthorpe. The introduction of steam power to the breweries did, however, assist the local metalworking industries, albeit at the expense of the woodworking trades on which the equipment had traditionally depended.

Other industries included soap-making (making over 1.5 million lb of soap in 1845) and the manufacture of agricultural implements including the new steam engines. Colman's established themselves in

Carrow in 1858, making mustard, flour, blue and starch. Paper-making and printing became a major employer and it is perhaps symbolic that Jarrolds took over the old Yarn Mill in 1902. But such industries still employed only a small proportion of the Norwich workforce. A large number were in domestic service; others were still engaged in personal trade, or in the large but dispersed, building industry.

The road transport system developed in the early nineteenth century but the real stimulus to economic development came with the railways, offering speed and a lowering of costs. East Anglia was initially slow to develop its system – due to the 'apathy and inertness' of the local people 'to their own salvation' according to a letter in the *Norwich Mercury*, but Norwich eventually had three stations. Thorpe station was built in 1844 for the Yarmouth and Norwich Railway (and rebuilt in 1886); Victoria station (1849) was outside St Stephen's Gate; and the City station (1882) was outside Heigham Gate. The railways brought coal from the Midlands, cattle from Ireland, and exported the products of local industry. The siting of the railways also shifted the focus of transport routes within the city. To serve Thorpe station properly it was first necessary to widen London Street and Castle Street, and then to construct, as a speculative venture in 1860, a new street to avoid the congestion of Rose Lane/Prince of Wales Road. The station also encouraged new development in the surrounding area – terraces for the railway workers, hotels and factories. Elsewhere in the city the communication system was opened up.

The introduction of the railways played a major role in bolstering the city's economy from the mid-nineteenth century. The original Thorpe railway station was built in 1844 and rebuilt in 1886. Its presence led to considerable development in the surrounding area. This view by J. Newman in 1844 shows Foundry Bridge in the foreground, before its rebuilding in 1885

The Post Office building on Prince of Wales Road was built in 1865, originally as a bank

Davey Place (1812) and Exchange Street (1829) were both built out of old inn yards off the market and followed the construction of Little Bethel Street in 1792 as the start of a new development of the street system.

One of the best views of Norwich's nineteenth-century heritage comes from walking up Prince of Wales Road. Leaving Thorpe railway station of 1844, one crosses the rebuilt Foundry Bridge of 1885 and rises up to Agricultural Hall Plain; thence past Harvey's Crown Bank of 1865 (later the post office), the Agricultural Hall of 1882 (Anglia House) and the Royal Hotel (1897). Below the castle mound is Shire House, which dates in its present form from the 1820s.

The Improvement Act of 1806 introduced (albeit slowly) cambered and paved (cobbled) streets, which were partly financed by the adjacent householders. By 1850 the streets were lit by gas. Bridges were rebuilt. Law and order was improved, with a new police force of eighteen constables and a superintendent being introduced on the London model from 1836, and gradually incorporating the earlier 'watch'; there were eighty officers by 1851. Initially the police also combined the duties of firemen, but in 1847 a city fire brigade was established. This was with the encouragement of the Norwich Union Insurance Company whose own company fire service (not finally disbanded until 1858) had been one of the mainstays of fire protection until then. Private brigades operated by other companies such as Colman's and

Boulton and Paul continued to supplement this municipal brigade well into the twentieth century.

But for all these improvements the nineteenth century in Norwich was also a time of squalor. By 1848, a fifth of the population of Norwich were described as paupers who were 'scarcely able to provide their families with bread and much less able to supply them with fire and sufficient clothing'. A 'winder' in the weaving industry might only receive 2*s* per week – if employment could be found. Indeed, the Health of Towns Commissioners believed that Norwich's days as a commercial and manufacturing centre were over and that the city would revert to being an agricultural market.

The better off artisans were moving out into the new suburbs but the poor continued to live in crowded tenements built within tightly-enclosed yards. In 1910 there were 710 such courts in the city. The poor ventilation and sanitation contributed to the spread of typhoid, cholera and other diseases. In some areas there was no drainage and the filth ran along surface gutters. In others, sewers from the tenements led into communal cesspits in the centre of the yards. A court in St Paul's (White Lion Court) contained twelve houses, a stable and a slaughter house; there was a communal privy but the filth oozed into an open rubbish bin adjacent, and sometimes even into the houses as their floors were lower than that of the yard. In the 1860s one family elsewhere, consisting of mother, father, a son of twenty-one and daughters of fifteen and twenty-nine all slept in a room 12 ft by 7 ft 9 in. The son eventually died of typhus but was kept in the room for a further three days while the father and mother (who also had the disease) continued to sleep there. The water supply was described by a health inspector in 1850 as being 'bad in everything that should constitute a water supply' while the city surveyor simply described the Wensum in 1864 as 'presenting all the features of a large sewer'. It is therefore perhaps not surprising that Norwich had one of the highest mortality rates in the country. A quarter of deaths in 1873 were of the under fives. The inhabitants took solace where they could. A third of the numerous public houses were known to be common brothels!

The development of the nineteenth-century suburbs was a radical departure from Norwich's history. They consisted of both large speculative housing developments for artisans and higher quality developments for the better off. Crook's Place, west of St Stephen's Road, was the first attempt to provide a low-cost estate, with rentals of £4 to £8. It comprised about 250 houses built along three streets (Chapel Street, King Street and Queen Street) with long front gardens but narrow communal yards. Some estates were truly massive, such as the

Many of the medieval courtyard developments, poor in their day, were foul slums by the nineteenth century . (*W. Chambers, 1875*)

View down Cowgate towards Whitefriars Bridge in 1834, just before the building of the Silk Yarn Mill. Jarrold's Printing Works is now on the left

Sandringham Improvement area between Dereham Road, Earlham Road and Heigham Road between 1861 and 1897. The suburbs display interesting social stratification – from the exclusive developments such as Town Close estate (1873) off Newmarket Road to the better quality middle-class houses of the period built along the main suburban roads, lesser homes immediately off the side streets and with poorer houses behind those (as off Unthank Road, on Trinity Street and Cambridge Street).

The population of the city in 1871 was 80,386. In 1980 it was 180,000 but during the same period the death rate had almost halved. The late nineteenth century is notable for the range of improving legislation that greatly benefited the quality of life in the city (although it was resisted initially by some as interference with personal liberties!). It was achieved through the introduction of radical new powers to the

Norwich's 'other' cathedral, the Roman Catholic St John's on Earlham Road, was built 1884–1910 on the design of George Gilbert Scott. It is built adjacent to a series of chalk mines that date back at least to the sixteenth century

council. The first medical officer of health was appointed in 1875 and this signalled a revolution in the administration of health care. The medieval drainage system was at last replaced by the first sewer, laid in 1869. The first slum clearance programme began in 1877. In 1889 the Corporation acquired powers to compel the owners of the many courts and yards around which the poorer quality tenements were built to drain and pave them. New building was to be regulated (minimum room height was to be 8 ft, with 150 ft of open space at the rear – effectively forbidding back-to-back houses) and council houses could be built.

In many ways, therefore, the twentieth century opened on a very different Norwich. Of not least significance in view of Norwich's long history of involvement with the textile industry is the fact that in 1901 there was not a single worsted weaver left in the city.

CHAPTER THIRTEEN

The Modern City

The start of the twentieth century saw major changes in the look of the city. If the nineteenth century became the age of the railways in Norwich then the twentieth century started as the age of the tram. Whole streets were removed in Castle Meadow and around Orford Place, and awkward bends altered. In return the Tram Company paid for the re-paving of many of the city's streets. When the trams first ran in 1900 it created a festival occasion, in which 'Women forgot all modesty' according to contemporary newspapers and 'leaned out of bedroom windows whilst still wearing their hair curlers'!

Despite the improvements in public health and housing conditions from the last quarter of the preceding century, early twentieth-century Norwich was still wracked with its long-standing poverty. But the citizens were now able to vent their frustration with a new political voice. It is not surprising that Norwich took a leading part in the rise of the

The Royal Arcade was built in 1899 by George Skipper. It is a superb example of Art Nouveau building

Labour Movement and elected a socialist MP in 1905. Another notable step foward was the election, in 1923, of Dorothy Jewson as the city's first female MP. A member of the influential local family, she had been born in 1884 and was educated at Norwich High School and Girton College, Cambridge. She joined the new Independent Labour Party and, after serving (1923–4) as MP, she was a member of the National Council of the ILP until 1935. She also served as a City Councillor until 1936. A programme of slum clearance in the 1920s and '30s followed the Addison Act of 1919 which offered local authorities subsidies to help build the new houses that they needed after the First World War. Other legislation followed in the 1920s and 1930s but this radical programme was then halted by the Depression. These efforts were coupled with trying to provide other work for the unemployed. By 1933 there were 7,000 men out of work (from a total population of 128,000). Public works included parks such as the James Stuart Gardens off Prince of Wales Road (1922), Wensum Park (1925) and that at Eaton (1928), council housing estates (the first being at Mile Cross dating from 1918–23) and the construction of the new City Hall on the west side of the market-place in 1938. Before its construction the councillors claimed that they had been forced to carry out business in rat-infested ex-public houses around the market-place!

The First World War had an immense personal effect on the people of Norfolk – one in nine of the 100,000 servicemen involved was

The Norwich Union building on Surrey Street is one of the city's finest Edwardian buildings. It was built in 1903–4 by G.J. Skipper. The growth of the Norwich Union group of insurance companies has been one of the most significant developments in the nineteenth- and twentieth-century economies of the city

A turn of the century view of wherries beside the wharves along King Street, overlooked by Black Tower on Butler Hills. Note the vent of the malthouse on the left of the picture. (*Original print by William Buston*)

killed. One of the heroes of the conflict was the Norwich nurse, Edith Cavell, who was executed in October 1915 for trying to help British and French prisoners to escape the Germans. (Her memorial is outside the east end of the cathedral). But the effect on the home front was more limited. The Norfolk and Norwich Hospital was used to treat the many casualties from the Western Front and the city was frequently crowded with troops on their way for embarkation. It was the fear of the Zeppelin raids that seemed to bring the war to Norwich's doorstep. A blackout was imposed which went to the extreme lengths of people wearing luminous buttons to avoid collisions after dark.

The Second World War brought a greater horror – the Blitz. In over forty-four air raids from June 1940 to 1943, 340 people were killed and 1,092 injured. In one incident a crowded public shelter dug within Chapelfield Gardens took a direct hit. Over 30,000 houses and 100 factories were damaged, and seven of the city's medieval churches were destroyed. After a long 'phoney war' there were a number of 'hit and run' raids from June 1940, and in April 1941 one raid made a direct hit on Colman's works. Worse was to come. Norwich had been picked out for two of the *Baedecker* raids in April 1942. These deliberately chose towns of historic interest as targets but Norwich also had important war industries, notably Laurence and Scott's and the heavy engineering of Boulton and Paul. Other local firms had also adapted to the war effort: the last surviving silk manufacturer, Francis Hinde and

Son, made parachutes. The first raid came on the night of 27 April and lasted two hours. In all, approximately 180 high explosive and up to 7,000 incendiary bombs were dropped. The last air raid came on 6 November 1943 although the city was later attacked by the V1 and V2 rockets. Colman's took spectacular precautions and dug extensive air raid tunnels, which could accommodate over 1,000 people, in the adjacent cliff. An 80 ft high observation tower was built near the top of Carrow Hill to warn of approaching daylight bombers.

The 1950s was a period of rebuilding from the war damage, although many bombed sites remained open for much longer. Many, however, would argue that the 1960s saw a second 'blitz', as many historic buildings and whole streets were demolished in the name of progress and in the hope of attracting future prosperity. Unfortunately the period came to be symbolized by the construction of office blocks that few appeared to actually want. This was a trend that was not peculiar to Norwich but

Norwich City Hall was built in 1932–8 by C.H. James and S.R. Pierce. It has been held to be one of the foremost English public buildings constructed between the wars. The north wing was never completed

affected many historic towns in the country. Other changes were brought about by the need to accommodate the motor car. Large areas were cleared in the Theatre Street area for car parks, and the construction of the north part of the Inner Ring Road (St Crispin's Road) destroyed Stump Cross and blighted Magdalen Street, effectively cutting off St Augustine's and arguably leading to a depression there that still continues. St Stephen's Street and Westlegate were among those other streets whose appearance changed out of all recognition. One consequence of the level of destruction was the realization that there was an urgent need to rescue the archaeology of the city before it was gone forever. Thus was the Norwich Survey project born. It excavated over forty sites between 1971 and 1978, and the results radically altered our appreciation of the history of the city. One symbol of the way planning controls have developed is that an awareness of archaeological needs is now seen as an integral part of the planning process in the city.

The most devastating damage to Norwich during the Second World War was caused by the *Baedecker* raids of April 1942. Here we see the aftermath along St Benedict's Street

Economically, the traditional textile industry continued its long decline during the twentieth century and the last silk mills were finally closed down in 1980. But since the Second World War a number of new enterprises have been attracted to the city. These include the chemicals industry (May and Baker from 1958) and the University of East Anglia from 1963. In 1968 part of Her Majesty's Stationery Office (HMSO) moved to the newly-built Anglia Square development off Magdalen Street in order to take advantage of the lower rents and costs outside London, and as part of a move towards government decentralization. In the 1970s, 61 per cent of the working population was engaged in the service industries, with the largest single employer in the city being the Norwich Union. Another 34 per cent was engaged in the manufacturing industries. Of the latter, the two largest categories were shoe-making (with twenty-two shoe factories making over

Norwich ablaze! Botolph Street shortly after an air raid

A lost Norwich streetscape: view up Westlegate, looking towards All Saints' church at the turn of the century. The 'Barking Dickey' public house is top left

16 per cent of all British shoes) and food and drink, notably Colman's Foods at Carrow and Rowntree Mackintosh (ex-Caley's) off Chapelfield Road. The largest single manufacturing employer was the engineering firm of Laurence, Scott and Electromotors Ltd. Newer industries were sited on the outskirts of the city off the new outer ring road, as were the massive domestic suburbs that rapidly grew up: the commuter belt now takes the impact of Norwich far beyond its official City boundaries. A danger in this type of development on the fringes is that the centre becomes deserted and derelict, and efforts have been made in Norwich to arrest this process with new developments alongside the river, such as Peel Mews beside Coslany Bridge. Another is a block of student residences off Coslany Street, innocently or impishly called Mary Chapman Court – after the person who founded the Bethel Hospital in 1713 'for the habitation of poor lunatics'.

The pattern of communications has also changed greatly in the city. Rail transport has deteriorated since the closure of two of the city stations while the river – once the heart of the communication network – is now primarily used as a leisure resource. A new facet to the communications system has been brought by the building of a regional airport on the old RAF airfield at Horsham St Faiths, opening up rapid international communications via Amsterdam. Norwich is also now a centre for television production for both the BBC and Anglia TV, another aspect in which the city is regional capital.

One important new source of revenue is the heritage that has been the inspiration for this book. Thousands of visitors flock to see the cathedral, the churches, the many museums and the picturesque buildings such as Elm Hill. Large hotels have been built to serve the visitors. At the time of writing a large shopping mall is in the process of construction on part of the site of the old castle. Whether or not the latter will prove an asset, or an eyesore, to the historic landscape is something that posterity must judge. The building work was preceded by extensive archaeological excavations which were generously funded by the developer. But present government and archaeological policy would stress that excavation should only be a matter of last resort, with a preference for finding design solutions that would allow the archaeological remains to be preserved *in situ* for the benefit of future generations. The heritage is an attraction but it is also a tremendous responsibility and it is often difficult to find suitable uses for buildings that can only properly be preserved by keeping a function that is appropriate to the twentieth century – although they have layouts designed for a different age (as, for example, Nos 2–4 Lion and Castle Yard). A particular concern is the preservation of upper floors and

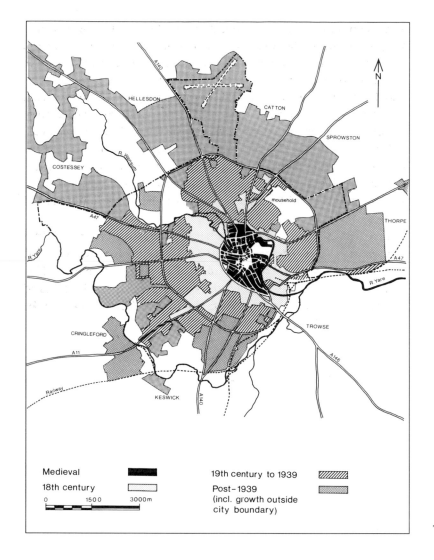

The expansion of Norwich

roofs of buildings for which only the ground floor has a perceived commercial value. The Old Barge on King Street is undergoing long-term restoration as a heritage centre but one cannot simply turn all historic buildings into museums. The most obvious success story is that of the restoration of Elm Hill. It now seems almost inconceivable that this major tourist attraction was only saved from demolition as a slum by the casting vote of the mayor in 1924. Great efforts have also had to be made to find workable uses for the large numbers of churches that became redundant and therefore risked decay. Uses have ranged from night shelter, Scout HQ, community, martial arts and antiques centres, and a puppet theatre. As important as the individual buildings is the streetscape in which they were built. The difficulty of maintaining these within the walled city has been made easier by the recent trends towards pedestrianisation schemes (as the highly successful London Street and Gentleman's Walk). This creates its own problems in the need to funnel traffic around the edges of the historic city. Fortunately the distinctive outline of the medieval city is still largely preserved, and it is hoped that future relief roads around the margins of the ancient city will continue to respect that element of the townscape. Indeed, in 1970 a Council report on the city walls stressed that 'the line of the wall will be a positive feature clearly defining the old city.'

The terminal date of this history has been chosen as 1974, as in this year, as part of the reorganization of Local Government, Norwich lost its status as a county borough and became a district council. This transferred some powers to the county council and marked the end of an era in Norwich's history – but it has done nothing to diminish the status, and our affection, for this 'fine city'.

Map of walk route

A Walk through Norwich's Past

A s you walk around Norwich remember that the line of the streets themselves as much as the buildings that lie beside them is an important signal from the past.

The tour is designed so that it can be divided into a number of routes of differing lengths. It also contains a number of churches and museums en route that are well worth taking a longer time over. The map also shows other places of interest that you may wish to visit.

It is a tour punctuated with fine medieval churches. It used to be said that in Norwich there was a church for every week of the year and a pub for every day. The small 'tippling houses' have now gone (although there are still plenty of public houses) but most of the churches do still remain, although many have had to find new uses.

The tour starts in the commercial heart of the Saxon town in the market-place of Tombland.

This was the site of the market, and heart of the eleventh-century planned Saxon town. Tombland means 'empty' land. At the south end was the earl's palace (the present public lavatories reputedly mark the site of its chapel), towards the centre was St Michael's church – the wealthiest church in Saxon Norwich and at the north end (under the Maid's Head Hotel) was the Norman bishop's palace. The emplantation of the cathedral was used by the Normans to affirm their stamp of authority on the Saxon town. A Saxon street originally ran through the site of the precinct, beside what is now the Erpingham Gate, towards a major crossroads on which was possibly the church of Holy Trinity. The Norman cathedral was built directly over that crossroad.

A medieval market continued to be held here and was the subject of bitter disputes between the citizens and the cathedral over who had the

WALKING TOUR

right to the tolls or market fees. In 1272 this erupted into a full scale riot. The north gate into the Close (Erpingham Gate) was built by Sir Thomas Erpingham as a thanksgiving for his survival at the battle of Agincourt in 1415. The buildings lining the precinct wall of the priory are all post-medieval encroachments on to the former open market.

On the west side of the street is Augustine Steward's house (No. 14), built c. 1530 and occupied by the rebels during Kett's rebellion of 1549. Note the shield on the corner of the building which carries the merchant's mark of Steward. This building was prefabricated before final erection. If you go down the alley that runs beside it you will see numbers scratched into the first floor timbers so that it could be properly reassembled. The Samson and Hercules, now much restored, dates back to 1657.

Go north down Wensum Street, past SS Simon and Jude's church to Fye Bridge.

The medieval name of Wensum Street was Cook Row, and there were probably eating houses and certainly a meat market here. At the

The tour starts in Tombland which is itself a palimpsest of Norwich's history. You stand in the Saxon market, beside a Roman road. To the east is the great cathedral precinct, symbol of the power of the Norman church and state – and source of many a medieval dispute with the city. The buildings built on to the wall of the precinct are good post-medieval examples of encroachment into the former open space of the city

The sixteenth-century merchant's mark of Augustine Steward, as found on his houses on Tombland and Elm Hill

top of the street is the Maid's Head Hotel. This is a fine example of a nineteenth-century coaching inn but also incorporates fragments (a possible cushion capital) of the late eleventh-century bishop's palace. The road going off to the right is Palace Street, a new street of 1318 necessitated by an extension of the cathedral precinct to accommodate a new bishop's palace. The church of SS Simon and Jude was a Saxon foundation and possibly once the bishop's chapel. The present building dates to the fourteenth/fifteenth century – a time at which most of the Norwich churches were rebuilt. Fyebridge was the site of a Saxon ford across the river and leads into the heart of Middle and Later Saxon Norwich. On the opposite bank of the river, along Fishergate, excavation has revealed evidence for Saxon reclamation of the foreshore in the tenth/eleventh century. Fyebridge Street, leading into Magdalen Street was the street that ran through the centre of the tenth-century defended town. This was the heart of the original Northwic. The Mischief Tavern dates back to 1312.

Pass by the church of St Clement and turn left on to Colegate.

St Clement is probably another Saxon foundation but no evidence of the original fabric remains. This street contains fine examples of seventeenth- and eighteenth-century houses. On the south side of the road is the remains of a substantial sixteenth-century flint house (now much altered offices). Beyond it are two of the finest early eighteenth-century houses in the city. Note the date of 1743 on the rainwater head. The street also contains superb examples of the strong nonconformist tradition in Norwich, in the shape of the Old Meeting House of 1693 and the Octagon chapel of 1754–6, both on the north side of the street.

On your right you will pass the two parallel streets of Calvert Street and St George's Street.

These still mark the line of the tenth-century defences of Saxon Norwich. The 2 m (6 ft) deep and 8 m (24 ft) wide defence ditch ran along St George's Street, while Calvert Street marks the line of a street running behind the rampart. Note the 'dog's leg' of the crossroads between the two arms of Colegate beside St George's Street. This possibly represents a misalignment as an attempt was made to join a street from each side of the still standing rampart. Between Calvert Street and St George's Street is Bacon's House. This is a fine example of a late medieval merchant's house, built by stages to eventually form a courtyard plan with a timber-framed upper floor carried on a flint-walled ground floor. The church of St George Colegate dates from the twelfth century. It contains the fine early sixteenth-century terracotta tomb of Robert Jannys. **If you divert slightly and walk along St George's Street** you will come to the much-restored house of William Watson, (a late seventeenth-century weaver), one of the few surviving examples of a weaver's cottage.

Return to Colegate and walk towards St Michael's church.

The remarkable flint flushwork on the south aisle and chapel is original and dates to the early sixteenth century, although that on the south and east walls of the chancel is a good copy of 1883–4. Behind you is a restored seventeenth-century cottage with good examples of a weaver's large dormer windows. You are now at the south end of the Middle Saxon settlement of Coslany. This means, literally, 'island in a bog'. The settlement stretched south to north from St Michael's to St Martin at Oak and was probably joined to the defended circuit of Northwic in the eleventh century.

Turn south along Coslany Street.

You are now walking through what was once a very marshy area but which was occupied by horn-workers in the eleventh/twelfth century. The river was the key to industrial activity in this area. It was first used to soak the horns but then played a major role in the operation of the dyeing industry. **As you pass over Coslany Bridge** notice Peel Mews, to your right, which is built over the site of a number of tenements that contained dyehouses dating back to the twelfth century. **You will now come on to Westwick Street**. This was originally 'Letesteres Row', a reference to the dyeing industry. To the left are the remains of a later Norwich industry – Bullard's Anchor Brewery dating back to the 1860s. This is one of the few survivors of the heyday of Norwich brewing in the nineteenth century, when at its peak there were twenty-three breweries. Look up to the late fifteenth-century St Laurence's church – a rebuild of the original of 1038–66. It is perched precariously on the slope of the gravel terrace above the edge of the river marsh. This is a measure of the determination of a Saxon landlord to build a church on his land and so take a share of the tithes! **Walk up through the alleyway that runs beside its tower** and pause to look at the carving in the spandrels beside the entrance to the church. On the left is St Laurence being roasted alive on a gridiron. On the right is King Edmund of East Anglia being tortured by the Danes.

You will now pass on to St Benedict's Street.

This was originally the line of a Roman road leading to Brundall. There are five churches along its quarter mile length, as it spread as a ribbon development in the late Saxon and Norman period. But although the density of early churches gives a good indication of the pattern of landholdings, it does not necessarily reflect the same density of domestic occupation. A great deal of land at the west end of the street (by St Benedict's church) was farmland until the fourteenth century.

Walk east towards Charing Cross.

On the right is St Gregory's church, now dating in the main to post-1394 but with its square tower encasing Saxon work. This church was built just outside the bounds of the eleventh-century town, probably as the principal church of the suburb. Charing Cross – 'Shearing Cross' – was the place around which medieval cloth cutters and shearers would gather hoping for employers to give them work. The cross itself was demolished in 1732. On the right is Strangers Hall. The origin of the name of this medieval mansion, despite the association of Norwich with the 'Strangers', is unknown. The oldest part of the building dates back to the 1320s and buildings were later amalgamated to form a courtyard house. It is now a folk museum.

Pause at the junction of Charing Cross with St John's Alley.

On the opposite side of the road at the junction with Duke Street, the present multi-storey car park marks the site of the sixteenth-century palace of the Duke of Norfolk. It was rebuilt in 1602 and again in 1671, when it contained sixty hearths as well as its own bowling alley. In front, note the view across the valley of the Great Cockey and the rise up St Andrew's Hill. The Roman road curved around to the left to pass under the cathedral, the spire of which is visible behind Blackfriars church (St Andrew's Hall).

St John's Street leads to the church of St John Maddermarket.

The name reflects the market selling dyes which was sited here. Madder gives a purple-red dye. At the foot of the churchyard, uncomfortably close to the piled-high graves, is one of the few surviving parish pumps. This was the principal source of water for the poor of the parish until the late nineteenth century. At the top of St John's Street is Pottergate. This was named after the presence of Saxo-Norman pottery kilns concentrated on the east end of the street (Kiln House to the west is a modern naming without archaeological evidence). The earliest kilns lay within the area of the Late Saxon town on Bedford Street (to the east) but later ones spread out into this suburban area and may date as late as the twelfth century. Evidence for kilns has been found both on Lobster Lane and on the end of Dove Street.

Turn up Dove Street and into the market-place.

You are now in the Norman Borough built in the late eleventh century on the outskirts of the late Saxon town. This became the commercial heart of the medieval town, with its importance reflected in the presence of two of Norwich's finest monuments.

The Guildhall, 1414–35 (with modifications in 1535 and 1861), is the largest medieval city hall built outside London and was clearly built to impress the visitor with the status of Norwich. It is built of flint rubble carefully faced with knapped flints, the spaces in between filled with flint chips in a style called 'galleting'. The stonework of the east gable is treated with lozenge and triangular chequerwork of flint and freestone. The style was later taken up more elaborately in some of the city churches.

St Peter Mancroft is often mistaken by visitors for the cathedral. It was completely rebuilt in the space of twenty-five years, from 1430.

The market here was the main provisions and crafts market for the city. It has been possible to reconstruct the layout of the rows of stalls. But in the seventeenth century and later a feature of the scene was the 'ped market' where farmers' wives would sit on the cobbles with their produce displayed in semicircular baskets or 'peds' in front of them.

Gentleman's Walk was originally Cordwainer's Row, where one of the main concentrations of pre-fourteenth-century shoemakers lived. It became a fashionable place to promenade in the nineteenth century, hence its modern name.

Turn down Royal Arcade (or Davey Place when the arcade is closed) into Back of the Inns and left down Castle Street.

Royal Arcade, built in 1899, was originally the entrance through the medieval Angel Inn. It leads to the Back of the Inns, the name of which derives from the fact that it served as the rear entrance to the coaching inns facing the market-place. Davey Place was created by Alderman Davey in 1812 by demolishing the King's Head. A noted republican, he had mischievously created a storm by announcing that he was to 'put a hole in the king's head'. The line of Back of the Inns and Castle Street marks the course of a stream or cockey that flowed through the centre of the street and was used as a sewer, being crossed by a number of footbridges. It was the boundary of the castle fee. Note how the road continues to curve around into London Street, still following the line of the castle defences.

Cross into Swan Lane and thence to Bedford Street.

You are now back in the Saxon town. A Saxon pottery kiln was found at No. 21 Bedford Street during rebuilding work. No. 15 Bedford Street still retains rare elements of a sixteenth-century shopfront. The jambs of the door survive together with the lower parts of mullions from the flanking unglazed windows. The bottom part of the shutters for these windows would have been lowered to make a table for the display of sales goods, while the upper part of the shutter would have provided an awning. Look down Bedford Street and note the dip in the street which marks the course of the Great Cockey.

The Bridewell was originally a fourteenth-century merchant's house, built for Norwich's first mayor, William Appleyard. The walls are among the best examples of flintwork in the city. The fine joints between the regularly cut blocks have been filled with slivers of flint – a technique called 'galleting'

Pass into Bridewell Alley and on to St Andrew's Street.

The Bridewell was built in 1370 and was the home of William Appleyard, the first mayor of Norwich. It is a splendid example of fine flintwork with the narrow joints between the cut flint filled with slivers of flint, known as 'galleting'. It takes its name from its sixteenth-century use as a prison for beggars and vagrants. The building is now a museum. At the bottom of the street is St Andrew's church, a 1478–1506 rebuild of a late eleventh-century original. Across the street, low-lying on the former marsh, is the medieval Blackfriars of 1440–70. Behind it stands part of the surviving cloisters, with some excavated remains laid out for view. This is one of the finest urban friary complexes in the country.

Follow the road up St Andrew's Hill on to Redwell Street.

Garsett House faces St Andrew's Plain and is a fine timber-framed building. The lower floor was an early sixteenth-century shop with the upper floor a rebuild of 1584: note the date on the corner bracket. Note also on the south side of the building a rare survival of an insulated fixture that supported the tramlines of the early twentieth century.

Suckling House on the right is a much modified early sixteenth-century merchant's house. Pause at the top of the hill. Over to the right is Queen Street. This contains the small church of St Mary the Less. Now completely built around, this thirteenth/fourteenth-century church was given to the French Strangers in 1564 as a trading hall for their cloth. In the seventeenth century it became the French church. Directly opposite you is the church of St Michael at Plea.

Now walk down Redwell Street and pause at the junction with Princes Street.

St Peter Hungate church museum is on the corner. The line of Princes Street was diverted in the twelfth century when St George's church was built. The street originally ran to the left of the church tower. On the corner of Princes Street is No. 6, built *c.* 1619. Princes Street, off to the right, contains a restaurant with a fine fourteenth-century undercroft and a good group of sixteenth-century jettied buildings.

Continue down the hill and turn right into Elm Hill.

If you pass down the hill you will see the east end of Blackfriars with fourteenth-century Becket's chapel to your left. Pause in the open space beside the Briton's Arms, have a rest and admire one of Norwich's premier townscapes – but this fine view of medieval and later buildings was only saved from demolition as a slum by the casting vote of the mayor in 1924. The Briton's Arms dates from the fourteenth century and was originally a 'Beguinage' for a community of religious women. It then became an inn, The King's Head, but in 1804 it was forced to change its name as a result of republican fervour during the French Revolution.

All but one of the rest of the medieval buildings of the street were destroyed in the disastrous fire of 1507. As you walk along the street you will see how the buildings were progressively rebuilt up to *c.* 1520. It is not just the fronts of the buildings that are impressive. **If you go down Strangers Club Yard** you will see the backs of the houses. Note the great variety in the positions of the fireplaces as each builder experimented with the recent introduction of built fireplaces. These replaced the more fire-prone open hearths and hoods of the medieval period. **Return to Elm Hill** and you will see another fifteenth-century survivor of the fire in No. 41, Pettus House, built with timber framing and an open gallery on the first floor. No. 26 has the framing infilled with brick nogging. The occupant of No. 28 wished to hide the timber framing completely in the eighteenth century and concealed it behind a cladding of wafer thin 'mathematical tiles'. The Little Gallery, dated to 1670–90, on the left, is the only building on the street that dates from after the 1520s reconstruction. Note the characteristic brick string course.

> **You will now pass right, back up Wensum Street towards Tombland and the cathedral.**

What better place to end this tour than with Norwich's masterpiece, the cathedral, in front of you. To visit this constitutes a tour in its own right. Do not simply look at the church but appreciate it within the setting of its precinct – a town within a town. The complex contained living quarters, stables, workshops and a brewery. A canal ran up from Pulls Ferry to bring building stone to build the cathedral itself. In the main it is a splendid Norman and later achievement. But if you look at the west wall of the Infirmary (next to the coffee shop) you will see a row of round 'Saxon' windows that suggests the presence of local masons, who were able to express traditional styles on what were considered lesser elements of the job.

Further Reading

Primary Sources
The most easily accessible source for historic records regarding the city is:
W. Hudson and J.C. Tingey (eds), *The Records of the City of Norwich*, 2 vols (Norwich, 1910)

Secondary Sources
The following general accounts deal with the history/archaeology of the city generally or deal with specific aspects of it.
C. Barringer (ed.), *Norwich in the Nineteenth Century* (Norwich, 1984)

J. Campbell, *Norwich* (fascicle from *Historic Towns* vol.1 ed. M.D. Lobel, London, 1975)

R. Gardiner, *The story of Norwich Cathedral* (Norwich, 1987)

B. Green, *Norwich Castle, A Fortress for Nine Centuries* (Norwich, 1970)

B. Green and R. Young, *The Growth of a City* (Norfolk Museums Service, 2nd edn., 1981)

R.W. Ketton-Cremer, *Norfolk in the Civil War* (Norwich, 1969)

J. Pound, *Tudor and Stuart Norwich* (Chichester, 1988)

U. Priestley, *The Fabric of Stuffs* (Centre of East Anglian Studies, UEA, 1990)

H. Sutermeister, *The Norwich Blackfriars* (Norwich, 1977)

Archaeology

Detailed reports on the results of archaeological excavations in Norwich are contained in volumes of *East Anglian Archaeology*. Of especial note is the volume on finds from excavations:

S. Margeson, *Norwich Households* (Norwich Survey/Norfolk Museums Service)

Summary accounts of archaeological excavations have appeared in the following:

M. Atkin and S. Margeson, *Life on a Medieval Street* (Norwich Survey, 1985)

B.S. Ayers with A.J. Lawson, *Digging Under the Doorstep* (Norfolk Museums Service, 1983)

B.S. Ayers, *Digging Deeper* (Norfolk Museums Service, 1987)

B.S. Ayers *et al, Digging Ditches* (Norfolk Museums Service, 1992)

An annual round-up of recent finds is contained within the journal *Norfolk Archaeology*

For a photographic record of Norwich in the late nineteenth and twentieth centuries see: M. Colman, *Norwich in Old Photographs* (Stroud, 1990)

Places to Visit

T he visitor is advised to check locally for details of opening and any charges. The Tourist Information Office is located in the Guildhall, Guildhall Hill (0603 666071).

Bridewell Museum, Bridewell Alley. Displays of Norwich crafts and industries (667228).

Castle Museum. The castle dates back to the twelfth century and houses a range of displays covering the archaeology of the city and region (223630).

Carrow Priory, Carrow Works (by appointment). A small museum telling the history of Carrow Priory and the history of the Colman's factory.

Cathedral. Contains an exhibition on the history of the cathedral.

Church Museum, St Peter Hungate Church, Princes Street. Displays of church art and craftsmanship.

Colman Library, Norwich City Library, Esperanto Way. Reference collection of books on local history and archaeology, together with old photographs.

Dragon Hall, King Street. A fifteenth-century house containing a remarkable medieval crown post roof including a carved dragon. In process of conversion to a heritage centre (663922).

Jarrold's Printing Museum, Whitefriars. Within medieval undercroft (660211).

Norfolk Records Office, Norwich City Library, Esperanto Way. The primary source for many documents relating to the city.

Regimental Museum, Shire House. The history of the Norfolk Regiment.

Strangers Hall Museum, Charing Cross. Deals with aspects of everyday life in post-medieval Norwich, set within a medieval merchant's house (667229).

Telephone Museum, St Andrew's Street. A specialist museum on the history of the telephone (661714).

Many of the medieval churches in the city are now locked due to vandalism. See locally for details of entry.

Acknowledgements

My first thanks must go to the late Alan Carter who, as Director of the Norwich Survey from 1971 to his tragic death in 1988, was the endearing, if at times frustrating, inspiration for many of us. He is sadly missed.

Thanks also to all of my former colleagues in the Norwich Survey, Norfolk Museums Service and Centre of East Anglian Studies (University of East Anglia). These include Philip Andrews, Susanne Atkin, Gill Baker, Mavis Bithray, Martin Creasey, the late Peter Donaldson, Dave Evans, Barbara Green, Prof. Hassell Smith, Sarah Jennings, Philip Judge, Mary Karshner, Serena Kelly, Sue Margeson, Bill Milligan, Ursula Priestley, the late Jan Roberts, Robert Smith, the late Helen Sutermeister and Margot Tillyard. And not least to the teams of local volunteers who gave so much to both the excavation programme and to the documentary research. A particular thanks is also owed to Brian Ayers, Jayne Bown and the other staff of the Norfolk Archaeological Unit for their assistance in providing information on the most recent finds. Many of the illustrations are from the collections of the Norfolk Museums Service and I am grateful to the director, Mrs Catherine Wilson, for permission to reproduce them. Thanks also to Peter Crowe, Antiquarian Bookseller, for supplying a number of the prints used in this book. The debt that this book owes to the inspiration of *Growth of a City* by Barbara Green and Rachel Young will be obvious. This was a true milestone in the popularization of Norwich history and archaeology.

A final thanks must go to my wife, Susanne, whom I first met on a dig in Norwich.

Illustrations on pp. 4, 6, 7, 13, 19, 60, 68, 69, 71 are copyright courtesy of Norfolk Museums Service (Archaeology Dept); p. 84, Norfolk Museums Service (Bridewell Museum); pp. 17, 18, 20, 25, 26, 35, 36, 49, 53, Norfolk Museums Service (Norfolk Archaeological Unit); pp. 16, 45, 61, 62, 72, 73, 74, Norwich Survey. The photographs by George Swain on pp. 101, 102 are copyright Judy Ball. The reconstruction on p. 76 is by Wayne Laughlin. The illustration on p. 27 is by permission of the Society of Antiquaries of London.

Index